The Europe

HETTNER-LECTURES

Series editors:
Hans Gebhardt and
Peter Meusburger

Managing editor:
Michael Hoyler

Volume 10

Department of Geography
University of Heidelberg

The European geographical imagination

Hettner-Lecture 2006
with
Michael Heffernan

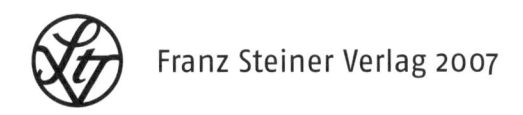

Franz Steiner Verlag 2007

Bibliografische Information der Deutschen Nationalbibliothek
Die Deutsche Nationalbibliothek verzeichnet diese
Publikation in der Deutschen Nationalbibliografie;
detaillierte bibliografische Daten sind im Internet über
<http://dnb.d-nb.de> abrufbar.

ISBN 978-3-515-09096-4

Jede Verwertung des Werkes außerhalb der
Grenzen des Urheberrechtsgesetzes ist unzulässig
und strafbar. Dies gilt insbesondere für Übersetzung,
Nachdruck, Mikroverfilmung oder vergleichbare
Verfahren sowie für die Speicherung in Datenver-
arbeitungsanlagen.
© 2007 Franz Steiner Verlag, Stuttgart
Druck: Printservice Decker & Bokor, München
Printed in Germany

Contents

Introduction: Hettner-Lecture 2006 in Heidelberg   3
PETER MEUSBURGER and HANS GEBHARDT

Prologue   7
MICHAEL HEFFERNAN

Capturing Europa: images, narratives, maps   17
MICHAEL HEFFERNAN

European dreaming: France, Britain and the new Europe, c. 1914 - c. 1945   41
MICHAEL HEFFERNAN

The new cosmopolitanism: European geographies for the 21st century   63
MICHAEL HEFFERNAN

The Klaus Tschira Foundation gGmbH   91

Photographic representations: Hettner-Lecture 2006   95

List of participants   101

INTRODUCTION

Introduction: Hettner-Lecture 2006 in Heidelberg

Peter Meusburger and Hans Gebhardt

The Department of Geography, University of Heidelberg, held its tenth and last 'Hettner-Lecture' from 12 June to 16 June 2006. This annual lecture series, named after Alfred Hettner, Professor of Geography in Heidelberg from 1899 to 1928 and one of the most reputable German geographers of his day, is devoted to new theoretical developments in the crossover fields of geography, economics, the social sciences, and the humanities.

During their stay, the invited guest-speakers present two public lectures, one of which is transmitted live on the Internet. In addition, several seminars give graduate students and young researchers the opportunity to meet and converse with an internationally acclaimed scholar. Such an experience at an early stage in the academic career opens up new perspectives for research and encourages critical reflection on current theoretical debates and geographical practice.

The tenth Hettner-Lecture was given by Michael Heffernan, Professor of Historical Geography at the School of Geography, University of Nottingham. A past editor of the leading *Journal of Historical Geography* (1996-2005) and author of *The Meaning of Europe: Geography and Geopolitics* (1998), Michael Heffernan is internationally renowned for his research on the history and politics of geography from the 18th century to the present, and his work on the inter-relationship between geography, landscape, war and memory.

During the Hettner-Lecture 2006 Michael Heffernan presented two public lectures entitled 'The rise and fall of the European geographical imagination' and 'Europe in the 21st century: geography, hospitality and refuge'.[1] This book contains the reworked version of the material presented in Heidelberg in the form of an introductory statement and three substantive essays. Seminars with graduate students and young researchers from Heidelberg and seven other European universities took up issues raised in the lectures. These were entitled 'Geographies in/of Europe', 'Geographies of asylum', and 'Violence places: warfare and the geographical imagination'.

Overall, 328 students and post-docs from 60 universities in 17 countries took part in the Hettner Lecture seminars over the past ten years. 282 young researchers came from 34 German universities, and 46 participants originated from Switzerland (11), Hungary (8), Great Britain (7), Austria (6), USA (3), Israel (2), Russia (2), Canada (1),

---

[1] 'The rise and fall of the European geographical imagination', *Alte Aula der Universität*, Monday, 12th June 2006, 18.15; afterwards reception. 'Europe in the 21st century: geography, hospitality and refuge', *Hörsaal des Geographischen Instituts*, Tuesday, 13th June 2006, 15.15. The second lecture was followed by a public discussion, chaired by Matthew Hannah (Vermont).

China (1), Croatia (1), Estonia (1), France (1), Japan (1), Norway (1) and Spain (1). The international character of the seminars greatly enriched the debates among participants and has led to the establishment of lasting cross-border networks. In many universities, the Hettner Lectures have contributed significantly to the renewed intensification of theoretical debate in geography.

We should like to express our gratitude to the *Klaus Tschira Foundation* for generously supporting the ten Hettner-Lectures between 1997 and 2006. Particular thanks are due to Dr. h.c. Klaus Tschira, our benevolent host in the *Studio* of the foundation's magnificent *Villa Bosch*. After ten years we decided to conclude the Hettner Lectures and start a new innovative project that focuses on interdisciplinary aspects of 'Knowledge and Space'.[2] We also thank Prof. Dr. Peter Comba, Vice-Rector of Heidelberg University for his welcome address at the opening ceremony in the university's *Alte Aula*.

The Hettner-Lecture 2006 would not have been possible without the full commitment of all involved students and faculty members. We thank Jana Freihöfer, Tim Freytag and Heike Jöns for the planning and chairing of the seminar sessions, and Kathrin Heinzmann und Jana Freihöfer for their effective organisational work. We are immensely grateful to all students who assisted with the organisation of the Hettner-Lectures over the past ten years. Finally, we would like to thank Michael Hoyler for his excellent work as managing editor of the ten volumes of this book series, and his indispensable conceptual and organisational input to the Hettner Lectures.

---

[2] See http://www.knowledgeandspace.uni-hd.de/

PROLOGUE

Prologue

Michael Heffernan

A few years ago, I received a fax from a double-glazing company based in Mansfield, an English industrial town to the north of Nottingham, the city where I live and work. One of the managing directors of this company had discovered my details on the web and was seeking my 'expert' advice on a question he believed an academic geographer with a professional interest in Europe should immediately be able to answer. He wanted to know whether a district on the northern outskirts of Istanbul was in Europe or not. Intrigued, I immediately telephoned the number on the company notepaper. An entertaining conversation ensued. The managing director wanted to be able to charge the appropriate amount for a delivery of windows in connection with a major new housing development. Company regulations specified a European delivery rate, implying but without mentioning the EU, and a more expensive rate for deliveries beyond Europe. He wanted to charge the lower, European rate to encourage further business but his less generous co-director was determined to charge the higher, non-European rate. My interrogator knew Turkey wasn't in the EU but that was true of lots of other places in the eastern part of Europe, a region he deemed to be unproblematically 'European'. He was especially conscious of the fact that Turkish soccer teams took part in UEFA competitions and that one such team had recently won the UEFA Cup itself. The EU was important, he conceded, but why not use UEFA's more expansive definition of what he called 'geographical Europe' rather than the version specified by 'the bureaucrats in Brussels'?

He was initially nonplussed that I wasn't able to resolve this apparently straightforward problem with a simple answer but we spent an interesting 20 minutes discussing the changing idea of Europe over the past few centuries, with particular reference to Turkey and with entertaining diversions on the history and geography of European soccer competitions and, in a surreal moment, the Eurovision song contest which had recently been won by a trans-sexual Israeli. Did this mean, wondered the managing director, that the Middle East was also part of what he suddenly started calling, rather wonderfully, 'the people's Europe'? At the end of the conversation, my interlocutor felt he had enough information to convince his less generous colleague. I'm not sure whether he was successful but I was delighted to receive a subsequent email saying he had just purchased a copy of a book I wrote a few years ago on this general topic.[1]

---

[1] Michael Heffernan, *The Meaning of Europe: Geography and Geopolitics* (London: Arnold, 1998).

I begin with this anecdote because it goes to the heart of what I want to do in the three essays that make up this volume.[2] These essays provide geographical commentaries on different aspects of the 'European debate' from its origins in the 17th century to the present. The European debate is defined as that long-standing and on-going interrogation of the essential characteristics and core principles that might determine what it means to be European. This debate has drawn on a set of foundational narratives that emerged during the course of the 17th, 18th and 19th centuries. Some of these narratives, which collectively constitute a kind of continental mythology, are discussed in chapter one, which also reviews how this European mythology has engendered a particular conception of space – a European geographical imagination.

The concept of a European geographical imagination owes much to the closely related idea famously developed by Edward Said in his pioneering discussion of the European invention of the 'Orient', a region roughly equivalent to the Middle East. According to Said, European travellers, writers and academics who described the Middle East from the 18th century onwards were involved, often unconsciously, in a process of geographical creation and appropriation. In Said's analysis, Europe is presented in rather monolithic and undifferentiated terms as a pre-existing locus of economic and military power but I want to suggest that the imaginative process he describes with respect to the Middle East also took place in Europe itself. Europe too was created by a European geographical imagination rooted in the same nexus of power and knowledge that Said identifies.[3] Europeans not only constructed versions

---

[2] The first and third of these essays were delivered as the 10th Hettner Lectures in Heidelberg in the summer of 2006, the former in the University's Alte Aula, the latter in the Department of Geography. I was delighted and honoured to be asked to deliver these lectures, the last in the sequence, though I was rather overwhelmed by the responsibility of following so many distinguished scholars who have contributed to this series in the past decade. My anxiety, which occasionally bordered on panic, was eased, however, by the wonderful support and hospitality I received from friends and colleagues in Heidelberg who had previously welcomed me into their midst as an Alexander von Humboldt Research Fellow in 1999-2000. The lectures and seminars took place during the best World Cup soccer competition in living memory, hosted by Germany, and this provided both welcome diversion and an unexpected topic for debate in the seminars. I owe a great debt to Peter Meusburger, doyen of Heidelberg geographers and a scholar to whom the international community of geographers owes an incalculable debt both for his own research and for the work he has done over many years to facilitate the free exchange of ideas across national boundaries. Hans Gebhardt was equally welcoming and I am equally grateful to him. Thanks also to Jana Freihöfer, Tim Freytag and the many students from across Europe who brought such energy and vitality to the seminars. Heike Jöns and Michael Hoyler, long-standing friends and now colleagues at Loughborough University in the UK, were extremely helpful before and after the lectures. I am especially grateful to Michael for his patience and support in recent months.

[3] Edward W. Said, *Orientalism* (London: Penguin, 1978) pp. 49-73 and his later analysis in Edward W. Said, *Culture and Imperialism* (London: Chatto & Windus, 1993). The concept has also been developed by Derek Gregory in ways that increasingly converge with Said. See his *Geographical*

of other regions to legitimise their colonial domination of these spaces; they also and simultaneously constructed their own space.

The European debate has been the central driving force behind this process, though the enthusiasm for thinking and writing about Europe in terms of its core values and principles has waxed and waned. In general, the European debate has been at its most intense during episodes of crisis and warfare, notably so in the 20th century. In chapter two, I consider some French and British contributions to the European debate in the years between the wars, an era when liberal democracy was under continuous and serious threat. This was a remarkably fertile period for the European debate as writers, academics and intellectuals sought reasoned responses to economic collapse and the rise of totalitarian regimes and ultra-nationalism. After World War Two, in the era when concrete manifestations of European economic and political integration at last began to emerge in the form of international treaties, intergovernmental agencies, and pan-European organisations, the debate about the nature and meaning of Europe became strangely muted and prosaic, even in the writings of Jean Monnet, Robert Schuman and the other architects of European Union. Before 1945, the idea of European unity was discussed and legitimised in sweeping cultural terms; after 1945, the same idea was more readily expressed in the practical, managerial language of trade, commerce, economics and security.

The European debate has been gathering momentum once again since the end of the Cold War and the ensuing re-configuration of the European political landscape in the 1990s. Chapter three considers this latest phase in the debate and argues that the renewed impetus has continued since 2000 as consequence of EU enlargement and the events of 11th September 2001. The expansion of the EU to encompass nearly 500 million citizens across 27 countries (over 300 million of whom now share a single currency) poses obvious questions about the cultural and political values that might conceivably unite this vast arena. The transformation of American foreign policy since 2001, particularly (though not exclusively) towards the Muslim world, and the recent US and British invasions of Iraq and Afghanistan have also prompted a remarkable outburst of new thinking in many parts of Europe about the possibility of an independent European foreign policy that might counterbalance an American stance that seems at odds with the majority European public opinion, a fact

---

Imaginations (Oxford: Blackwell, 1994); 'Imaginative geographies', *Progress in Human Geography* 19 (1995) pp. 447-485; 'Power, knowledge and geography', in *Explorations in Critical Human Geography. Hettner Lecture 1997* (Heidelberg: Department of Geography, University of Heidelberg, 1998) pp. 9-40; 'Edward Said's imaginative geographies', in Mike Crang and Nigel Thrift (eds.) *Thinking Space* (London: Routledge, 2000) pp. 302-348; and *The Colonial Present* (Oxford: Blackwell, 2004) pp. 17-20. The argument developed here on the relationship between geography and Europe also owes much to Dipesh Chakrabarty's analysis of the discipline of history in his *Provincializing Europe: Postcolonial Thought and Historical Discourse* (Princeton: Princeton University Press, 2000).

underlined by the massive public demonstrations against the invasion of Iraq in February 2003.

The most recent calls for a distinctive European foreign policy have been articulated in surprisingly expansive terms, with philosophers such as Jürgen Habermas and Jacques Derrida taking an unexpected lead in the public debate.[4] I will discuss the contributions of Habermas, Derrida and others in detail in chapter three but suffice it to say here that this latest phase in the European debate has re-focused attention on the ethical principles that might define a new European political culture in the 21st century. Several writers have attempted to flesh out a realistic political programme based on these initial discussions, including Ulrich Beck, Edgar Grande and Anthony Giddens. They have emphasised the need for a new European-style cosmopolitanism, based on the traditional Kantian ideal formulated at the end of the 18th century but updated to confront the new challenges of a global 21st century.[5] The arguments developed in favour of a new cosmopolitanism have arisen in part from a growing disillusionment with the liberal social and political policies developed from the 1960s onwards in the name of 'multiculturalism', a concept now widely believed to have encouraged rather than diminished ethnic and cultural segregation in Europe and North America.[6] In contrast to a multiculturalism that merely accepts cultural difference as a legal right but does little to prevent cultural antagonism, a truly cosmopolitan society defined by Beck and others would place greater responsibilities on all communities and individuals to communicate, integrate and thereby foster new and more dynamic political cultures that are premised upon the existence of evolving social and cultural differences rather than *a priori* and unchanging social and cultural norms. A self-consciously European 'cosmopolitics' (to use a phrase coined by Pheng Cheah and Bruce Robbins) would therefore require all communities to be informed by, and to help develop, national and European political cultures that would be defined by their progressive policies towards the

---

[4] The key contributions to this debate can be consulted in Daniel Levy, Max Pensky and John Torpey (eds.) *Old Europe, New Europe, Core Europe: Transatlantic Relations after the Iraq War* (London: Verso, 2005).

[5] Ulrich Beck and Edgar Grande, *Cosmopolitan Europe* (Cambridge: Polity Press, 2007) and Anthony Giddens, *Europe in the Global Age* (Cambridge: Polity Press, 2007).

[6] For classic liberal critiques of multiculturalism in North America, see Arthur M. Schlesinger Jr., *The Disuniting of America: Reflections on a Multicultural Society* (New York: W. W. Norton, 1991) and Brian Barry, *Culture and Equality: An Egalitarian Critique of Multiculturalism* (Cambridge, Mass.: Harvard University Press, 2001). In a European context, recent debates in Britain – instigated in part by Trevor Phillips, the Chair of the British Commission for Racial Equality and a passionate opponent of multiculturalism – have been influenced, and to some extent confused, by the revelation that recent terrorist outrages in London were carried out by young British-born men who were completely estranged from the society in which they lived, a process Phillips believes to have been encouraged by the failed multiculturalism of the recent past. See Yasmin Alibhai-Brown, *After Multiculturalism* (London: Foreign Policy Centre Publications, 2000).

cultural differences within and between European societies, and between Europe and the rest of the world.[7]

This has been an intriguing discussion given the relative silence on these matters over preceding decades. But it is difficult to see how these ideas will filter into the wider public consciousness. The rejection of the EU Constitution by the French and Dutch electorates in the 2005 referendums, although clearly influenced by domestic politics and the specific character of the document under scrutiny, suggests that many Europeans still feel uncomfortable about unduly proscriptive statements about the nature of the European project, notwithstanding the policies of their own governments and the arguments of pro-European intellectuals who have insisted that a written constitution would give concrete expression to these wider debates.[8]

In fact, one could argue that public confusion about the latest phase in the European debate has generated some unexpected new divisions. The long and expanding list of 'new' European nations that have been granted EU membership since the end of the Cold War, and the equally extensive list of countries still clamouring for entry, implies that the people around the edges of 'old Europe' harbour few doubts about the pace and direction of the European project and recognise that their economic, political and cultural interests are best served by either re-asserting or establishing their 'European' credentials. Estonia's recent ratification of the very EU constitution rejected by the French and the Dutch electorates exemplifies this conviction. And yet the evidence of 'Euro-barometer' surveys in the 'older', western parts of Europe where the political culture has previously offered general, and often overwhelming, support for constitutionally agreed proposals emanating from the EU and its precursor organisations, suggests that the process of EU enlargement has itself become the main source of anxiety and dissatisfaction. We are thus faced with a troubling paradox: the 'new' Europeans from the former communist east enthusiastically hope to partake in a European dream fashioned in the western half of Europe only to find that many of their fellow Europeans from that region now openly question whether they want to be part of the same project.

These tensions and confusions vividly illustrate arguments recently developed by David Harvey in his critique of cosmopolitanism. According to Harvey, the new cosmopolitanism has failed to take seriously those stubborn geographical questions, what he calls 'the banality of geographical evils', that must be overcome if a genuinely cosmopolitan political culture is ever to be established, whether in Europe or elsewhere.[9] The 'disruptive spatialities' Harvey has in mind include not only those

---

[7] Pheng Cheah and Bruce Robbins (eds.) *Cosmopolitics: Thinking and Feeling Beyond the Nation* (Minneapolis: University of Minnesota Press, 1998).

[8] Jürgen Habermas, 'Why Europe needs a constitution', *New Left Review* 11 (2001) pp. 6-26.

[9] David Harvey, 'Cosmopolitanism and the banality of geographical evils', *Public Culture* 12, 2 (2000) pp. 529-564.

intensifying geographical divisions between rich and poor or between white and black that actually exist on the ground as a consequence of our economic system but also (and perhaps more importantly) the conceptual geographical divisions we carry around in our hearts and minds that reify and institutionalise cultural and political difference.[10]

The three essays in this volume are intended as modest contributions to this latest phase in the European debate, mindful of Harvey's critique and his insistence on the constitutive significance of geography for a revived cosmopolitanism.[11] They are not intended to provide a single, overarching narrative but are presented as discrete contributions that draw extensively – though not exclusively – on geographical writings about Europe, past and present. I hope this will not be seen as an exercise in disciplinary special pleading for I wish to argue, following Harvey, that there is an urgent need to re-focus the European debate on the essential geographical factors, both real and imagined, that will shape whatever political culture is formed within Europe in the future.

A non-determinist assessment of the role that geographical factors might play in shaping a future European identity has rarely been attempted in the past. Geographers themselves must share a large part of the responsibility for this state of affairs. In contrast to the discipline's leading practitioners between the wars, who are discussed in chapter two, remarkably few geographers from the current generation have contributed to the latest phase in the European debate. On the whole, geographers have simply assumed the existence of a continent called Europe and got on with the admittedly very important business of exploring its economic, social and political geographies. Europe, it would seem, is regarded as a kind of geopolitical given, a universally acknowledged regional framework that requires no analysis in and of itself.[12] The crises generated by EU enlargement and the widening breach between European and American perspectives since 2001 suggests that a more fundamental geographical re-thinking is both necessary and overdue.

The central argument of this volume can be easily expressed as follows: the changing idea of Europe has generated its own geographies on the ground and been associated with an evolving geographical imagination, a specific way of conceptualising, understanding and representing space which has provided, *inter alia*, the primary intellectual justification for the modern discipline of geography. In other

---

[10] Some would argue that social policies developed in the name of a liberal multiculturalism have exacerbated rather diminished these psychological divisions.

[11] Denis Cosgrove, 'Globalism and tolerance in early modern geography', *Annals of the Association of American Geographers* 93, 4 (2003) pp. 852-870 makes a good case to consider, and mobilise, a longer history of geography than Harvey suggests.

[12] See, however, Martin W. Lewis and Kären E. Wigen, *The Myth of Continents: A Critique of Metageography* (Berkeley and Los Angeles: University of California Press, 1997).

words, the modern idea of Europe and the modern discipline of geography have been closely interwoven and mutually constitutive intellectual projects. This is a simple enough observation but its implications have rarely been considered, either by historians of Europe or by historians of geography. The larger objective of these essays is to reflect on this hitherto unexamined relationship.

The connections between the idea of Europe and the idea of geography, though rarely acknowledged, are actually rather obvious for the problem of Europe is evidently rooted in its basic geography or, more particularly, in the undeniable geographical fact that Europe is not an identifiable or unproblematic space and certainly does not qualify as a continent in the strict sense of that term. As the undifferentiated western part of the Eurasian land-mass, the area Halford Mackinder identified as 'the world island' just over a century ago, Europe has never had any clear or agreed borders, especially to its east.[13] Europe's history can thus be read as an on-going attempt to define what it means to be European and to fix that identity on the map, usually in opposition to a series of non-European 'others' against which Europeans have defined themselves, a tendency Friedrich Nietzsche noted with characteristic perspicacity in the 1880s. Europe, Nietzsche claimed, is that 'small prominent peninsula which wishes at all costs to represent itself as "mankind's progress" with respect to Asia'.[14]

---

[13] Halford J. Mackinder, 'The geographical pivot of history', *Geographical Journal* 23 (1904) pp. 421-442.

[14] Friedrich Nietzsche, *Beyond Good and Evil: Prelude to a Future Philosophy* (Cambridge: Cambridge University Press, 2002) p. 52. Originally published in 1886.

CAPTURING EUROPA:
IMAGES, NARRATIVES, MAPS

Capturing Europa: images, narratives, maps

MICHAEL HEFFERNAN

Images

The term 'Europe' is one of the more mysterious and disputed 'keywords' in our vocabulary.[1] The origins and connotations of the word have been much disputed ever since it first entered the major languages of the region, some time in the 17th century, as a 'place-name' to describe the supposedly distinctive cultural and political characteristics of the peoples inhabiting the western part of the Eurasian landmass, the area bounded to the south by the Mediterranean Sea, to the west by the northern Atlantic Ocean, and to the north by the Barents Sea.[2]

The word 'Europe' is derived from the figure of Europa who enters the annals of Greek mythology in a well-known story. Europa was the beautiful daughter of Agenor, a Phoenician king who was one of the sons of Poseidon. According to the legend, Zeus was so besotted by Europa that he disguised himself as a white bull in order to seduce her. Assuming the form of a bull is not, on the face of it, the most obvious strategy to realise an amorous liaison with a young woman but it must have seemed like a good idea to Zeus at the time for he duly turned up, in full bull disguise, on the beach where Europa was cavorting with her handmaidens. Tempting the young princess onto his broad back, Zeus then swept her off to Crete where she bore him three children.

It is not immediately clear what this story, and more particularly the figure of Europa, has to do with the region we now call Europe. The confusion is all too evident when one considers some of the classic artistic representations of this strange tale from the era when the word 'Europe' first began to gain widespread currency. The most famous rendering of the story is probably the 1580 painting by Veronese housed in the Palazzo Ducale in Venice (Figure 1). This is an unashamedly erotic scene, or rather three scenes in one. The main action, on the left, shows Europa in a rapture of gay abandon being assisted onto the bull's powerfully muscled body by several female courtesans, a difficult manoeuvre that has produced what the American singer Janet Jackson would call 'a wardrobe malfunction' of Europa's voluminous dress.

---

[1] The same could be said of 'space'. See David Harvey, 'Space as a key word', in David Harvey, *Spaces of Neoliberalization: Towards a Theory of Uneven Development. Hettner Lecture 2004* (Stuttgart: Franz Steiner Verlag, 2005) pp. 93-115.

[2] See Denys Hay, *Europe: The Emergence of an Idea* (2nd ed., Edinburgh: Edinburgh University Press, 1968) and Peter Burke, 'Did Europe exist before 1700?', *History of European Ideas* 1 (1980) pp. 21-29.

Figure 1 Veronese's *The Rape of Europa* (1580)
(Palazzo Ducale, Venice)

As she clambers onto the bull, the huge beast is playfully licking one of her feet. In the mid-distant, Veronese shows the next scene in the story, a pantomime image of Europa and the bull swaying gently along a path through the bucolic splendour of a wooded glade towards the sea, her female assistants still dancing attendance. The third scene shows Europa waving back at her former companions on the shore as the bull swims powerfully out to sea.

Veronese's image is a story of seduction, to be sure, but it plainly reflects a mutual attraction between the two main protagonists. Indeed, the active and enthusiastic participation of Europa's handmaidens implies a joyful marriage ceremony rather than a kidnapping. The picture is undeniably charming and funny, despite its disturbing bestial connotations. The American novelist Henry James thought this painting was 'the happiest picture in the world… never did inclination and opportunity combine to express such enjoyment'.[3]

---

[3] Michael Wintle, *Europa and the Bull, Europe and European Studies: Visual Images as Historical Source Material* (Inaugural Lecture, Chair of Modern European History, University of Amsterdam, 2004) p. 14.

Figure 2 Titian's *The Rape of Europa* (1560)
(Isabella Stewart Gardner Museum, Boston)

Veronese's joyous and innocent image contrasts dramatically with Titian's depiction of the same scene, painted twenty years earlier and located today in the Isabella Stewart Gardner Museum in Boston (Figure 2). This is a much darker, violent and distressing portrayal and shows a rampaging bull plunging into the waves with a distressed Europa clinging for dear life to his horns while her friends scream in horror from the beach in the background. Titian's image fascinated later painters, including Rubens who painted an almost exact copy of the original seventy years later which now resides in the Museo del Prado in Madrid.[4]

But the most intriguing depiction of the Europa abduction is probably Rembrandt's 1632 painting, now in the Getty Center Los Angeles (Figure 3). This is a more complex, subtle and modern rendering of the scene, and the most troubling and sinister as a result. In Rembrandt's version, the action is caught at a specific moment

---

[4] See A. W. Eaton, 'Where ethics and aesthetics meet: Titian's Rape of Europa', *Hypatia* 18, 4 (2003) pp. 159-188; Margaret D. Carroll, 'The erotics of absolutism: Rubens and the mystification of sexual violence', *Representations* 25, 3 (1989) pp. 3-30.

Figure 3 Rembrandt's *The Rape of Europa* (1632)
(Getty Center Los Angeles)

when the bull heads out to sea with Europa seated on his back. She is glancing anxiously over her shoulder towards her female accomplices on the beach whose sudden concern for their mistress's well-being is all too obvious. The sense of surprise and bewilderment implies that the initial encounter with the bull had been playful and unthreatening but that events had taken an unexpected and worrying turn when the animal had seized its opportunity to carry Europa away. The bull is presented here as deceitful and cunning rather than violent and aggressive. The dominant impression is one of surprise and unease which merely hints at the full horror likely to unfold a few moments later when the bull's lustful intentions would become perfectly clear. In the distance, the coachman, in some ways the most disturbing figure in the painting and the only man to appear in any of these images, looks on impassively from the shadows. He had presumably escorted Europa and her handmaidens to the water's edge but he sits apart in his carriage in the dark woods, perhaps required to do so by his lowly status. He appears in any case strangely unmoved by the plight of the panic stricken women.

These very different versions of the Europa story all bear the same title: *The Rape of Europa*. This is an extremely disturbing idea to modern sensibilities though it evidently did not excite the same reaction in Veronese or any number of later artists who have recycled the image of Europa and the bull to represent the idea of Europe, either seriously or playfully, without dwelling on the distressing implications of the story. If the three representations of the Europa story discussed above can be taken as signifiers, they point to very different readings of the myth and, perhaps, of the very idea of Europe that this myth had recently come to symbolise in the 72 years that separate Titian's image from Rembrandt's. In Veronese, we have a joyful and playful representation of an encounter between two entirely different species, a woman and a bull, perhaps indicating the possibility of fruitful and harmonious exchange between the different peoples of Europe? In Titian, we are confronted with the abduction of a young and innocent woman by a brutal animal, a commentary, one might conclude, on the European capacity for spectacular violence? And in Rembrandt, we have a story of innocence and optimism betrayed, a distressing act observed with indifference by a negligent and silent witness, an observation, perhaps, on European cynicism and cruelty?

The lack of any consensus about Europe's essential characteristics, as revealed by these different images, does not appear to have been resolved with the passage of time. In fact artistic representations of Europe suggest that confusion about the region's essential characteristics intensified to the point where it becomes increasingly difficult to decide whether Europe was being represented by Europa, the bull, the union between them, or the setting in which their encounter took place. By the mid-19th century, the irony of an all-powerful Europe being represented by the helpless and pathetic figure of Europa was not lost on the generation of sculptors and artists who wished to depict the continent in stone or painting. For many, the bull rather than Europa seemed a more appropriate symbol for modern, confident Europe.

Sir George Gilbert Scott's recently restored Gothic revival memorial to Prince Albert, the consort of Queen Victoria, in London's Kensington Gardens indicates the new levels of complexity that the story had acquired at the height of the 19th century imperial age (Figure 4). At the four corners of the memorial, Scott commissioned different sculptors to create symbols of the world's continents in animal form, each surrounded by a group of human figures. Africa, Asia and the Americas are represented by the camel, the elephant and the buffalo, fairly obvious emblematic selections from the existing fauna of these continents, each surrounded by human figures in various postures and clothing. The focal point of the European group, created by the Ulster-born sculptor Patrick MacDowell, is a large, peacefully reclining bull on whose back sits the regal figure of Europa holding an orb and a sceptre. Four female attendants are seated around the bull, each representing a different European nation.

Figure 4 Patrick MacDowell's Europe, Albert Memorial, London (1875)
(Author's own photograph)

To the front sit France (depicted as Europe's military power, holding a sword and laurels) and Britain (presented as Europe's maritime and commercial power, holding a trident and with waves lapping at her feet). To the rear sit the two recently unified states of Italy (posed as Europe's centre of arts, with lyre and palette) and Albert's native Germany (Europe's centre of science and learning, holding a book). Needless to say, Europe is the only continent symbolized by reference to classical mythology and in which constituent nations have a clear and obvious presence. For Scott and MacDowell, it would appear that the rest of the world was the undifferentiated realm of nature; Europe was the home of placid Gods, albeit in animal disguise, protected by nations that collectively represent all aspects of the human condition.[5]

---

[5] For an extended study of the iconographic representations of Europe, see the outstanding forthcoming book by Michael Wintle, *The Image of Europe: Visualizing Europe in Cartography and Iconography throughout the Ages* (Cambridge: Cambridge University Press, 2008).

Narratives

In this section, I want to delve more deeply into the confusions, ambiguities and contradictions indicated by these various artistic representations.[6] Generalizing perilously, I want to suggest that five interwoven historical narratives can be detected as recurrent themes within the European debate. The significance of these narratives have waxed and waned over time, sometimes reinforcing one another, sometimes in contradiction. However, all five (and I admit that my list is not exhaustive) have ultimately fused to create the familiar image of Europe we carry around in our heads; the idea of Europe as home to an ancient and still unfolding civilisation.

Before discussing these narratives, two very important points should be emphasised at the outset. First, although there is a broad sense of chronology in what follows, I must emphasise that I am emphatically not arguing that themes presented in sequence here represent a kind of teleological historical progression whereby each of these versions of Europe has been supplanted and replaced by the next. Rather, and following the ideas developed many years ago by Michel Foucault, I present this simplified schema as a kind of 'genealogy' which recognises that ideas can and do combine and re-combine in complex ways in both time and space.[7]

Second, although each of these narratives can be, and often are, traced back to the most distant historical periods, to the ancient worlds of Greece, Rome or the early Christian era, they are in fact largely creations of the past four centuries. Europe, like so many of the concepts which shape our modern consciousness, is overwhelming an invention of the early-modern and modern periods from the 17th to 20th centuries. As Agnes Heller once remarked '[m]odernity, the creation of Europe, itself created Europe'.[8] Indeed, the first casualty of any analysis of the European debate is the comforting myth that Europe is an 'old' continent at the core of a global order of 'old' and 'new' worlds. But like so many essentially modern concepts, the power of the European idea lies precisely in the ability of those who have used this notion to project it backwards into periods when it had little or no meaning; to capture and then to mobilise the past, including the most ancient past, to legitimise particular views of Europe in the present and the future. Indeed, if I may be permitted to

---

[6] For related inquiries, see the essays in Kevin Wilson and Jan van der Dussen (eds.) *The History of the Idea of Europe* (Milton Keynes: Open University, 1993); Gerard Delanty, *Inventing Europe: Idea, Identity, Reality* (London: Macmillan, 1995); and Gerard Delanty, *Rethinking Europe: Social Theory and the Implications of Europeanization* (London: Routledge, 2005). The arguments developed here extend those proposed in Michael Heffernan, *The Meaning of Europe: Geography and Geopolitics* (London: Arnold, 1998).

[7] Michel Foucault, *The Order of Things: An Archaeology of the Human Sciences* (London: Tavistock, 1970).

[8] Agnes Heller, 'Europe: an epilogue?', in Brian Nelson, David Roberts and Walter Veit (eds.) *The Idea of Europe: Problems of National and Transnational Identity* (New York: Berg, 1992) pp. 12-25.

advance a definition of what it means to be modern, I would argue that it is precisely (and paradoxically) the capacity to control and manipulate the past.[9]

The first and perhaps oldest narrative is a religious-spiritual conviction belief that Europe was originally, and will in some measure always remain, an essentially Christian space. According to this story, an implicit association emerged after the collapse of the Roman Empire between *Christianimus*, the faith, and *Christianitas*, the geographical region in which this faith was predominant. This was, to all intents and purposes, the modern European world.[10] According to the standard accounts, a small, literate elite sharing a common Latin language inherited from the classical empire of Rome, common symbols and practices based on a pre-Reformation Catholic faith, as well as various pan-Christian cultural and educational ideals, created a 'continental ideology' slowly but inexorably over several centuries.[11] Within this Medieval Christian worldview, it is further argued, Islam was the original constituting 'other' against which Christians frequently united, particularly during the Crusades to win back control of the Holy Land, an episode that merely provoked further Islamic expansion into North Africa, Iberia and Anatolia. Christian Europe was a relatively homogenous but still highly vulnerable region, we are told, on the eve of the great voyages of discovery that would project European power into the New World. The Ottoman seizure of Constantinople in 1453, the fall of Belgrade in 1521, and the siege of Vienna itself ten years later demonstrate that Christian hegemony was by no means assured.[12]

Needless to say, recent research has challenged or undermined virtually every aspect of this story, though it retains a powerful grip on the popular imagination. The assault on the Christian narrative takes many forms.[13] First, it would appear that the concept of Europe seems to have had little or no geographical or other meaning for the classical civilisations centred on the Middle East and the Mediterranean basin and minimal significance even for the Roman Empire. The word 'Europe' is entirely absent from the Bible. While the term begins to be used alongside the more common geographical signifier of Christendom during the early Medieval period, its currency

---

[9] For a discussion of this idea in relation to the rise of the historical profession in the 19th century, see Hayden White, *Metahistory: The Historical Imagination in Ninteenth-Century Europe* (Baltimore: Johns Hopkins University Press, 1973) and Robert Gildea, *The Past in French History* (New Haven: Yale University Press, 1994).

[10] See, as a classic example, Hugh Trevor-Roper, *The Rise of Christian Europe* (London: Thames & Hudson, 1965), but also Jacques Le Goff, *The Birth of Europe* (Oxford: Blackwell 2005).

[11] Denys Hay, 'Europe revisited: 1979', *History of European Ideas* 1 (1980) pp. 1-6.

[12] The current vogue for counterfactual histories and novels have included some contributions that imagine how the world might have looked had Europe not asserted its global dominance. See, for example, Kim Stanley Robinson, *The Years of Rice and Salt* (London: Harper Collins, 2002).

[13] For a thoughtful review, see Ross Balzaretti, 'The creation of Europe', *History Workshop Journal* 33 (1992) pp. 181-196.

was limited though, revealingly, the word 'Europe' does appear regularly on Medieval manuscript maps.[14] Second, Christianity can hardly be regarded as a unifying force even before the Reformation and was anything but thereafter. The pre-Reformation Catholic Church was splintered by numerous schismatic forces through the early Medieval period and was in any case firmly divided between a Western Latin and an Eastern Byzantine church. The Reformation and the expansion of European power into the Americas during the 16th century created a complex mosaic of Catholic and Protestant communities which entirely undermined the idea of a unified and specifically Christian European space.[15] Third, the idea of Europe as defined in opposition to Islam has been also almost entirely overturned by a huge corpus of work on the cultural and intellectual exchanges between the Christian and Islamic worlds.[16]

Despite all this research, the original story of Christian Europe remains so familiar that it has acquired the status of poetically revealed truth; re-stating it is like reciting a catechism. It is surprising how influential this idea remains today, particularly in the current climate of marked Islamophobia. The hostility of many diehard Europeans (including leading European politicians such as Valéry Giscard d'Estaing) to the possible accession of Turkey to the EU has often been expressed in religious terms. From Giscard's perspective, it is simply impossible to imagine a European Union in which the largest country would have an overwhelmingly Muslim population.[17]

My second politico-legal narrative conceives of Europe in more secular terms as the region in which international law and political regulation were first invented during the Renaissance as an attempt to limit and control the territorial ambitions of emerging and rival nation-states. Europe, in this narrative, is the arena where a secure and permanent peace was deemed possible, though of course hugely difficult to establish. The Renaissance idea of Europe, as distinct from the pre-modern idea of Christendom, is deemed to rest on the Machiavellian notion of the balance of power as developed by theorists of natural law such as Hugo Grotius and as enshrined in the mid-17th century treaties of Westphalia that brought an uncertain end to the

---

[14] The literature on Medieval cartography is vast, of course, but Evelyn Edson, *Mapping Time and Space: How Medieval Mapmakers Viewed their World* (London: The British Library, 1997) provides a useful introduction. The full story is best approached via J. B. Harley and David Woodward (eds.) *The History of Cartography: Vol. 1 – Cartography in Prehistoric, Ancient and Medieval Europe and the Mediterranean* (Chicago: University of Chicago Press, 1987).

[15] Euan Cameron, *The European Reformation* (Oxford: Oxford University Press, 1991).

[16] See, as recent examples, Alex Metcalfe, *Muslims and Christians in Norman Sicily: Arabic Speakers and the End of Islam* (London: Routledge, 2003); Donald F. Lach, *Asia in the Making of Europe* (2 vols in 5 parts, Chicago: University of Chicago Press, 1965-1977); and Jack Goody, *The East in the West* (Cambridge: Cambridge University Press, 1996)

[17] For a discussion of Giscard d'Estaing's interview with *Le Monde* on Turkey, see the article on 'Europe: pour ou contre la Turquie', *Le Monde* 9 November 2002.

Thirty Years War. Threats to the Westphalian order after 1650, notably from Louis XIV's France, were represented as threats to what it meant to be European, particularly from the northern Protestant countries of the Netherlands and England. According to this narrative, the modern idea of Europe only gained currency in the late 17th century as a consequence of the Westphalia accords.[18] It was equated with the concept of a balanced system of sovereign nation states, each characterised by religious tolerance and expanding commerce. The idea Europe was not an alternative to the nation state; it was its guarantor.[19]

A politico-legal narrative has dominated the idea of Europe down to the present. The original idea of the balance of power was re-invented during the 19th century as the 'concert of Europe' to suit the very different and more complex geopolitical circumstances of that period but was still recognisably shaping the concept of Europe after the crisis of World War One when yet more proposals for a united, peaceful Europe were proposed, with their own distinctive geographies, by a new generation of pan-European theorists (see chapter two). By this stage, however, the visions of Europe were increasingly global, reflecting the obvious fact that most European powers had developed large overseas empires over the preceding two centuries. Europe was no longer merely defined as the locus of a balance of power between rival European states; it was also deemed to be the pivot of a global balance of power between emerging continental scale superpowers. The international Atlantic alliance that the European Union and its precursor organisations forged for security reasons after 1945 under the auspices of NATO can be regarded as simply the latest incarnation of an earlier idea of Europe as the pivot of a world-wide balance of power.[20]

The third cultural-intellectual narrative can conveniently be introduced by reference to the Duc de Sully's 17th century speculations on how to develop the Westphalia system into a genuinely united Europe. Sully's 'Grand Design', as it has generally become known to posterity, is still widely invoked as the foundational document of a united Europe. As a Protestant minister in the court of the French King Henri IV, Sully's design suggested a general European council (he considered locating this in Heidelberg) and also set down what he thought were the outer geographical limits of the secular Europe enshrined in the Westphalia system. For Sully, the Ottoman Empire had no part in Europe because international agreements ultimately rested on Christian values and these self-evidently did not apply in an Islamic realm. Sully's vision was, in this sense, entirely consistent with the first European narrative discussed above. However, Sully also insisted that Christian

---

[18] Burke, 'Did Europe exist before 1700?' *op. cit.*
[19] Michael Sheehan, *The Balance of Power: History and Theory* (London: Routledge, 1996).
[20] John W. Young, *Cold War Europe 1945-1989: A Political History* (London: Arnold, 1991).

Russia should be excluded from a future united Europe because he argued that the Russian people were essentially Asiatic in character and hence culturally inferior.[21]

This cultural dimension of Sully's proposal was highly significant because it exemplifies one of the fundamental contradictions at the heart of the European debate. At the very moment when Europe was defined politically in the most enlightened and inspirational terms as an arena where permanent peace might be established by international agreement, it was also defined geographically to exclude the peoples of other regions who were deemed culturally unworthy. It is difficult to over-emphasise the significance of this double process whereby Europe was defined according to the loftiest sentiments that were simultaneously used to exclude those deemed unable to live up to, or benefit from, these ideals.

Some of the subsequent proposals to ensure perpetual peace, as advanced by William Penn, John Bellers, the Abbé de Saint Pierre, Jean-Jacques Rousseau and Jeremy Bentham for example, challenged Sully's scheme and insisted that Russia and the 'slavic' peoples of the east had every right be to considered as part of the European 'family of nations' but this merely provoked equally counter-arguments in support of Sully's more exclusive original vision.[22] By far the most widely cited programme for European unity and perpetual peace was conceived by Immanuel Kant in the aftermath of the French Revolution, on the eve of the generalised warfare that would scar the lives of an entire generation of Europeans. Kant expressed a genuine interest in geography and one might have imagined that his programme would have been informed by a more sophisticated geographical sensibility. Sadly, although Kant's ideas are much in discussion as an early formulation of cosmopolitanism, they offered little serious challenge to the spatial exclusivities deployed decades earlier by Sully to define the outer European limits beyond which the perpetual peace and cosmopolitan harmony Kant sought would simply fail to apply.[23]

---

[21] There is a huge literature on Sully and the legacy of his Grand Design. See, for example, David Buisseret, *Sully and the Growth of Centralized Government in France 1598-1610* (London: Eyre and Spottiswoode, 1968) and Derek Heater, *The Idea of European Unity* (Leicester: Leicester University Press, 1992) pp. 15-38.

[22] Larry Wolff, *Inventing Eastern Europe: The Map of Civilization on the Mind of the Enlightenment* (Stanford: Stanford University Press, 1994).

[23] Kant's essay, 'Perpetual peace: a philosophical sketch', originally composed in 1795, is reproduced in Immanuel Kant, *Perpetual Peace and Other Essays* (ed. Ted Humphrey) (Indianapolis: Hackett Publishing Co., 1983) pp. 107-144. Recent discussions were sparked off by Martha Nussbaum, 'Kant and Stoic cosmopolitanism', *Journal of Political Philosophy* 5, 1 (1997) pp. 1-25, though see David Harvey, 'Cosmopolitanism and the banality of geographical evils', *Public Culture* 12, 2 (2000) pp. 529-564, for a spirited response on the failings of Kant's geographical vision, and also James Tully, 'The Kantian idea of Europe: critical and cosmopolitan perspectives', in Anthony Pagden (ed.) *The Idea of Europe from Antiquity to the European Union* (Cambridge: Cambridge University Press, 2002) pp. 331-358. See, as historical context for these debates, Margaret Jacobs, *Strangers Nowhere*

As a consequence of these debates, the eastern borderlands of Europe shifted back and forth, a process encapsulated by William Parker's memorable description of 'tidal Europe'.[24] Despite the efforts of westernising Russian monarchs such as Peter and Catherine the Great, both of whom insisted Europe's frontier lay along the Urals rather than on the western Russian border, by the mid-18th century the Russian east had replaced the Islamic south as Europe's principal constituting 'other'.[25]

This was not the end of the matter. As Michel Foucault once observed, one of the key inventions of the Enlightenment was the idea of population as something to be enumerated, classified, measured and assessed.[26] One consequence of this classificatory impulse was a re-definition of Europe as a cultural space whose frontiers would henceforth be measured according to a global assessment of the presumed (and sometimes spuriously measured) levels of civilisation of entire populations rather than their religious beliefs or the nature of the political regime that governed them. The question of defining European limits according to Enlightenment ideals therefore fused with a wider debate about the nature and limits of human progress and the legitimacy of imposing geographical limits on supposedly universal human rights. The European debate was thereafter expressed in an entirely new language in which words, previously unknown or used quite differently such as 'culture', 'civilisation' and 'progress', were much in evidence.[27] Despite powerful claims to the contrary, the freedom educated and cultured Europeans claimed for themselves in their hard-won battles against the tyranny of unelected rulers within Europe were not extended to the inhabitants of the vast spaces of Asia, Africa and the Americas whose lands were being colonised by Europeans. On the contrary, the continued existence of a tolerant, civilised, progressive European society in which such liberties and rights would be preserved seemed to imply the denial or even the active removal of these same rights from the colonised peoples of the non-European world. In a perilously circular argument, Europeans convinced themselves that they alone possessed the necessary and unique combination of virtues that both explained and legitimised their increasing global dominance. Thus was created what Michael

---

in the World: The Rise of Cosmopolitanism in Early Modern Europe (Philadelphia: University of Pennsylvania Press, 2006).

[24] W. H. Parker, 'Europe: how far?', *Geographical Journal* 126 (1960) pp. 278-297.

[25] Ivan Neumann, *Russia and the Idea of Europe: A Study in Identity and International Relations* (London: Routledge, 1996).

[26] Michel Foucault, *'Society Must be Defended': Lectures at the Collège de France, 1975-6* (London: Picador, 2003); Michel Foucault, *Sécurité, territoire, population: cours au Collège de France, 1977-1978* (Paris: Gallimard, 2004). This volume also includes an intriguing lecture on Europe (pp. 293-318).

[27] Michael Heffernan, 'On geography and progress: Turgot's *Plan d'un ouvrage sur la géographie politique* (1751) and the origins of modern progressive thought', *Political Geography* 13, 4 (1994) pp. 328-343.

Herzfeld has called the 'European self'.[28] The values of democracy, liberty and human rights shone so brightly in 18th century Europe partly because the rest of the world had been simultaneously and deliberately darkened. As Sigmund Freud once remarked 'It is always possible to bind together a considerable number of people in love, so long as there are other people left over to receive the manifestations of their aggression'.[29]

The fourth biological-environmental narrative was of an entirely different order and reflected an essentially 19th century, imperial definition of Europe. This was recognisably the offspring of 18th century debates about the cultural limits of Europe and was foreshadowed by the climatic and environmental debates of the Enlightenment, most notably through the writings of Montesquieu.[30] These ideas were re-cast during the 19th century in biological and environmental terms inspired by the growing enthusiasm for various forms of scientific racism backed up by theories of environmental determinism and, in the aftermath of the so-called Darwinian revolution after c. 1860, by the theories of 'social Darwinism'.[31] By the end of the 19th century, at the high point of the European imperial age, Europe was understood not as a region whose peoples had *acquired* a superior level of civilisation and hence had both a right and a duty to colonise the non-European world; rather, Europeans were deemed to possess an *inherent* racial superiority, often seen as a fortunate consequence of their supposedly benevolent physical environment. The continuation of this form of reasoning into the 20th century culminated with the tragic conviction that Europe's future would only be secured by eradicating long-established European communities in the name of a racially 'pure' Europe. If a 'dark continent' has ever existed, it was surely Europe between 1914 and 1945.[32] It would be comforting to think that this particular European narrative died out in 1945 but the recent resurgence of racism within Europe, directed towards other regions of the world and towards immigrant communities within Europe itself, suggests this idea of Europe is alive and well.

---

[28] Michael Herzfeld, 'The European self: rethinking an attitude', in Pagden, The Idea of Europe *op. cit.*, pp. 139-170.

[29] Sigmund Freud, *Civilization and its Discontents* (New York: W. W. Norton, 2005) p. 49.

[30] On Montesquieu's theories of environment and culture, one can do no better than return to Clarence Glacken, *Traces on the Rhodian Shore: Nature and Culture in Western Thought from Ancient Times to the End of the Eighteenth Century* (Berkeley and Los Angeles: University of California Press, 1967) pp. 501-705.

[31] See, for a readable introduction, Mike Hawkins, *Social Darwinism in European and American Thought, 1860-1945: Nature as Model and Nature as Threat* (Cambridge: Cambridge University Press, 1997). For a discussion of the same forces and their role on the development of modern geography, see David N. Livingstone, *The Geographical Tradition: Episodes in the History of a Contested Entreprise* (Oxford: Blackwell, 1992) pp. 177-259.

[32] Mark Mazower, *Dark Continent: Europe's Twentieth Century* (London: Allen Lane, 1998).

The fifth and final European narrative is couched in economic-technological terms and also originates in 18th and 19th centuries debates. Like the other narratives, the economic theories of Europe have also been projected backwards into a more distant Medieval or Roman imperial past when it is sometimes claimed that a pre-industrial integrated European economy existed. The rather different proposals for European unity put forward in France at the end of the Napoleonic wars by Claude-Henri de Saint Simon and Benjamin Constant were significant milestones in this discourse as both placed fresh emphasis on the power of economic, commercial and industrial relations, underpinned by new forms of science and technology, to overcome ancient political and cultural rivalries.[33] The early and mid-19th century doctrine of free trade, championed across Europe by Richard Cobden in the 1840s, was a recognisable development of these earlier formulations.[34] Most 19th century economic theorists, including Marx, accepted that in a mature industrial capitalist system, economic forces would ultimately overwhelm political and cultural divisions and create ever larger economic spaces, culminating in a single global economic order. The creation of a united Germany, though by no means a peaceful process of course, had clearly been driven by the logic of economic and industrial integration, backed up by transport technologies, stemming back to the creation of the *Zollverein* in the 1830s.[35]

The economic-technological narrative has remained a predominant theme within the idea of Europe since 1945, when actual pan-European political institutions finally emerged. This narrative has also been at the heart of debates between those who wish to limit Europe to an economic agenda and those who see this as no more than a necessary step on the road to federal political integration. This debate is possibly misguided, particularly if one believes the pioneering work by the British historian Alan Milward on the process of European economic integration after 1945. Milward

---

[33] Biancamaria Fontana, 'The Napoleonic Empire and the Europe of nations', in Pagden, The Idea of Europe *op. cit.*, pp. 116-128 and, more generally, Stuart Woolf, *Napoleon's Integration of Europe* (London: Routledge, 1991). Constant's pamphlet, published in 1813 and entitled *De l'esprit de conqête*, is reproduced in Biancamaria Fontana (ed.) *The Political Writings of Benjamin Constant* (Cambridge: Cambridge University Press, 1988). Saint-Simon's pamphlet, co-authored with Augustin Thierry the following year, was entitled *De la réorganisation de la société européenne, ou de la nécessité et des moyens de rassembler les peuples de l'Europe en un seul corps politique, en conservant à chacun son indépendance nationale* (Paris: Adrien Égron, 1814).

[34] For a fascinating discussion of the diffusion of the free trade doctrine, see Eric Sheppard, 'Constructing free trade: from Manchester boosterism to global management', *Transactions of the Institute of British Geographers* 30 (2005) pp. 151-172. On the supposedly peaceful implications of this doctrine, as defined by Cobden, see Daniel Pick, *War Machine: The Rationalisation of Slaughter in the Modern World* (New Haven: Yale University Press, 1993) pp. 19-27.

[35] See the classic economic analysis of German unification provided by Helmut Böhme, *Deutschlands Weg zur Grossmacht: Studien zum Verhältnis von Wirtschaft und Staat während der Reichsgründungszeit, 1848-1881* (Cologne: Kiepenheuer & Witsch, 1966). See also the excellent summary in David Blackbourn, *A History of Germany: The Long Nineteenth Century* (Oxford: Blackwell, 1997).

has concluded that the 'frontier of national sovereignty' was never seriously altered by the advent of the EEC and its successor institutions, a finding unlikely to please either side in this debate. Indeed Milward goes further and argues that despite the high-flying political and cultural rhetoric of the Treaty of Rome, the real emphasis has always been on technical solutions to practical problems determined by national interests: France's need for German raw materials, the Dutch need to secure the German market, Germany's need for international recognition, Britain's need for an 'escape clause' from economic ties and so on. According to Milward, the process of European economic integration preserved, rather than undermined, the traditional nation-states. Without the disciplines imposed by post-war European institutions, linked as they have always been to a North Atlantic military alliance, many western European nation-states would simply not have survived as liberal democracies after 1945 and would have collapsed under the weight of internal or external pressures. In Milward's admittedly controversial view, we should not be in the least surprised by the failure of European institutions to develop popular democratic accountability because their real purpose has traditionally been to bolster, rather than replace, the nation-states as distinctive and democratic structures.[36]

The same argument has been made by the US-based British historian Tony Judt who has noted that the process of post-war European economic integration was facilitated by wholly exceptional, never-to-be repeated circumstances. In Judt's view, it is most unlikely that Europe will ever again need 'to catch up on thirty years of economic stagnation or half a century of agrarian depression, or rebuild after a disastrous war. Nor will it be bound together by the need to do so, or by the coincidence of Communist threat and American encouragement. For good or ill the postwar circumstances, the midwife of mid-twentieth century Western European prosperity, were unique; no-one else will have the same good fortune'.[37] The rhetoric of post-war 'Europeanness' has thus been largely devoid of cultural or even political content, not least because it was based on a brutally imposed global geopolitical division that split Europe in two. The European project since 1945, though at last based on concrete institutional structures, developed in the looming shadow of the Soviet empire, the most monolithic and powerful of Europe's many constituting 'others'.[38]

---

[36] Alan S. Milward, *The European Rescue of the Nation-State* (London: Routledge, 1992).
[37] Tony Judt, *Grand Illusion: An Essay on Europe* (London: Penguin, 1996) p. 33.
[38] Neumann, Russia and the Idea of Europe *op. cit.*, pp. 131-141.

Maps

In working through these historical narratives of Europe, I have attempted, in rather general terms, to link each one to different real and imagined geographies, or at least to various external 'others' against which Europeans have defined themselves and their geographical domain. I now want to consider how the modern idea of Europe was itself a manifestation of new ways of conceptualising and understanding space. The European conception of space, created by the very process of European self-invention, is exemplified by geometrically ordered, discrete, bounded and controlled territory. This is what Derek Gregory has termed 'absolutist space', the clear, discrete space delineated by modern science and defined by modern law.[39] This is, in essence, the space of the modern map, which came in existence in order to display absolutist space. As David Buisseret reminds us, maps were extraordinarily rare before the Renaissance and there was accordingly very little capacity to read or understand them.[40] But the emergence of modern cartography was driven by the gradual shift from a pre-modern concept of space (in which the most important lines of communication were essentially vertical and spiritual between the individual and an imagined deity in the heavens) to a modern concept of space (conceived as a horizontal, bounded and secular territory). This signalled the need to survey, order and map land that was increasingly seen as private commodity rather than a common resource. The modern map both reflected and sustained the development of absolutist space.[41] The urge to map absolutist space, what has been called the 'cartographic imperative', has provided the primary rationale for the modern discipline of geography.[42]

The emergence of a European absolutist space and the consequential rise of cartography and geography were slow and gradual processes. As we have seen, most early modern visual representations of Europe were allegoric, symbolic and iconic

---

[39] Derek Gregory, 'Power, knowledge and geography', in *Explorations in Critical Human Geography. Hettner Lecture 1997* (Heidelberg: Department of Geography, University of Heidelberg, 1998) pp. 9-40, see pp. 15-22.

[40] David Buisseret, *The Mapmakers' Quest: Depicting New Worlds in Renaissance Europe* (Oxford: Oxford University Press, 2003).

[41] See, for different commentaries on this context, Alfred W. Crosby, *The Measure of Reality: Quantification and Western Society, 1250-1600* (Cambridge: Cambridge University Press, 1997); Denis Cosgrove, *The Palladian Landscape: Geographical Change and its Cultural Representations in Sixteenth-Century Italy* (Leicester: Leicester University Press, 1993).

[42] This phrase is borrowed from Anne Godlewska, 'Resisting the cartographic imperative: Giuseppe Bagetti's landscape of war', *Journal of Historical Geography* 29, 1 (2003) pp. 22-50. For intriguing commentaries on the rise of cartographic thinking in Europe, see Tom Conley, *The Self-Made Map: Cartographic Writing in Early-Modern France* (Minneapolis: University of Minnesota Press, 1996) and Christian Jacob, *The Sovereign Map: Theoretical Approaches in Cartography Throughout History* (Chicago: University of Chicago Press, 2006).

rather than cartographic.[43] The few 16th century maps that depicted large parts of Europe were usually navigational or portolan charts concerned essentially with coastlines rather than the continent's interior spaces.[44] However, the first printed atlases, also produced in the late 16th century, contained some of the earliest examples of printed maps of Europe contained in a single image and configured with respect to a new global order exemplified by the map projections developed by Gerard Mercator and others.[45] It is difficult to overemphasise the significance of these new cartographic images. They provided exceptionally powerful evidence that a space called Europe existed and that it was a discrete, bounded and ordered continent, just like its constituent nation-states that these same maps also displayed. Moreover, the structure of the atlases and the limitations of geographical knowledge about other continents inevitably meant that Europe emerged as the cultural and political core of the entire world. The most famous atlas map of Europe in this period is probably the one contained in Abraham Ortelius's *Theatrum Orbis Terrarum* of 1584, which contains a delightful motif showing Europa and the bull (Figure 5).[46]

---

[43] The connections and overlaps between these different kinds of representation are discussed in Wintle, The Image of Europe *op. cit*. See also Michael Wintle, 'Renaissance maps and the construction of the idea of Europe', *Journal of Historical Geography* 25, 2 (1999) pp. 137-165. As Wintle shows, while Titian, Veronese and Rembrandt were labouring over the paintings discussed above, other depictions of Europe as a noble female were being produced, devoid of bulls. Several of these images included motifs representing the rival European national spaces, often etched into Europe's flowing gowns. The most famous representation of a female Europe holding the balance of power can be found in Sebastian Münster's *Cosmographia Universalis* (Basle, 1588) folio xli. This image has been so widely reproduced as to be almost a cliché. It appears as a front cover of John Agnew, *Reinventing Geopolitics: Geographies of Modern Statehood. Hettner Lecture 2000* (Heidelberg: Department of Geography, University of Heidelberg, 2001) and is the frontispiece of Hay, Europe *op. cit*. It is interesting to ponder the different ways it is used and discussed in John Agnew and Stuart Corbridge, *Mastering Space: Hegemony, Territory and International Political Economy* (London: Routledge, 1995) p. 53; Pim der Boer, 'Europe to 1914: the making of an idea', in Wilson and van der Dussen, The History of the Idea of Europe *op. cit*., p. 52; Norman Davies, *Europe: A History* (Oxford: Oxford University Press, 1996) p. xviii; John Hale, *The Civilization of Europe in the Renaissance* (New York: Atheneum, 1994) p. 11; and Michael Wintle, 'Europe's image: visual representations of Europe from the earliest times to the 20th century', in Michael Wintle (ed.) *Culture and Identity in Europe: Perceptions of Divergence and Unity in Past and Present* (Aldershot: Ashgate, 1996) pp. 52-97.

[44] An excellent example is *Nova et exquisite description navigationum ad praecipvas*, held in the Salle des Cartes et Plans of Bibliothèque Nationale de Fance and discussed in Robert W. Karrow, *Mapmakers of the Sixteenth Century and Their Maps: Bio-Bibliographies of the Cartographers of Abraham Ortelius, 1570* (Chicago: University of Chicago Press, 1993) pp. 435-443 and pp. 660-1.

[45] Nicholas Crane, *Mercator: The Man Who Mapped The Planet* (London: Weidenfeld and Nicolson, 2002).

[46] The Ortelius map of Europe is from Abraham Ortelius, *Theatrum Orbis Terrarum* (Antwerp, 1584) Plate 2 (Europa) and has been reproduced and discussed in many places, including Jacob, The Sovereign Map *op.cit*., Figure 36, between pp. 268 and 269 and in Karrow, Mapmakers of the Sixteenth Century *op. cit*., pp. 1-31. The European map in Gerard Mercator's atlas of 1595 has

These representations still contain symbolic elements from earlier, Medieval conceptions of space but they describe a Europe poised on the brink of the Westphalian system, with each nation-state clearly represented, and therefore prefigure that more modern perspective.

Figure 5 Ortelius's Europe (1584)
(Abraham Ortelius, *Theatrum Orbis Terrarum*, Antwerp 1584)

Once the Westphalian system was established, the mapping of Europe changed fundamentally and remarkably quickly, beginning with the great surveys of France carried out by four generations of the Cassini family from the 1680s until the French Revolution under the auspices of the *Académie Royale des Sciences* in Paris. This long process, supported by three different French monarchs and privately raised funds, provided the template on which a geometric, absolutist space, a space now calculated by reference to astronomical measurement, spread across the face of Europe. This is a complex and fascinating story but it pivots around the first completion in 1718 of a narrow triangulated line around the meridian running through the Paris Observatory,

---

comparable significance. See *Atlas sive cosmographicae meditationes de fabrica mundi et fabricate figura* (Düsseldorf, 1595). This is reproduced and discussed in Crane, Mercator *op. cit.*, pp. 242-243. Some 102 of the 107 maps in Mercator's atlas deal with Europe.

the headquarters of the *Académie des Sciences*, from Dunkirk in the north of the country to Collioure in the south, an experiment initially designed to test different theories about the shape of the earth (Figure 6).[47] The language of the *Académie*'s report on

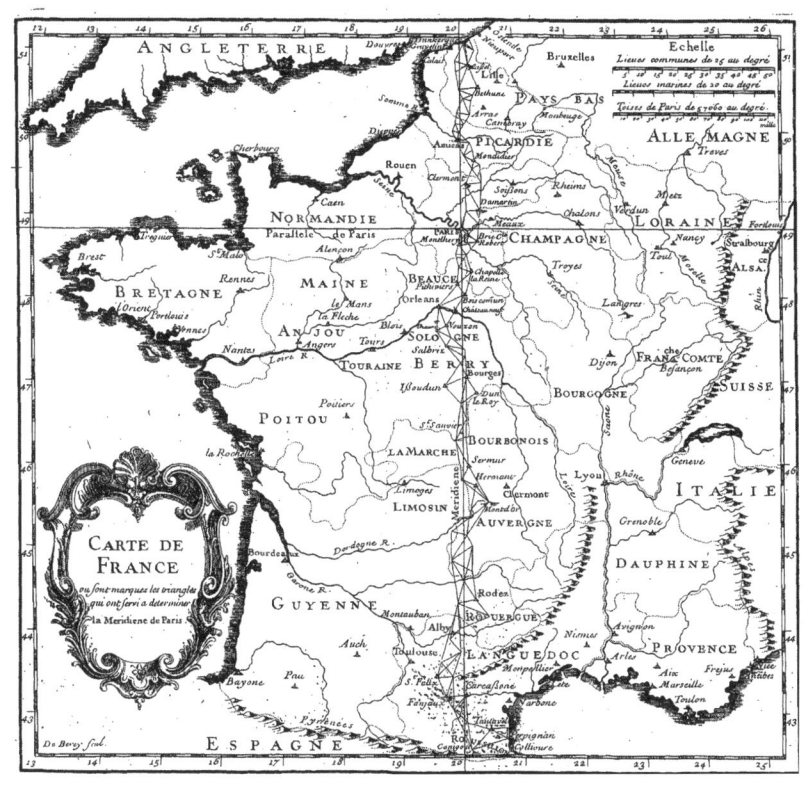

Figure 6 Paris meridian triangles (1718)
(Reproduced by permission of the Bibliothèque Nationale de France)

this survey, published in 1720, is precise and revealing: 'L'Académie Royale des Sciences a toujours regardé comme un objet digne de ses préoccupations tout ce qui peut contribuer à la perfection de la Géographie & de la Navigation'.[48] The objective was not merely to survey and then map the French national space set in its correct

---

[47] This map is entitled the *Carte de France en sont marquez les triangles qui ont servi a determiner la méridienne de Paris* and appears in Académie Royale des Sciences, *De la grandeur et de la figure de la terre: suite des mémoires de l'Académie Royale des Sciences: Année MDCCXVIII* (Paris: Imprimerie Royale, 1720) pp. 302-303. On the general story, see Monique Pelletier, *Les cartes de Cassini: la science au service de l'État et des regions* (Paris: Éditions du C.T.H.S., 2002); Josef Konvitz, *Cartography in France, 1660-1848: Science, Engineering and Statecraft* (Chicago: University of Chicago Press, 1987); and Mary Terrall, *The Man Who Flattened the Earth: Maupertius and the Sciences of the Enlightenment* (Chicago: University of Chicago Press, 2002).

[48] Académie Royale des Sciences, De la grandeur et de la figure de la terre *op. cit.*, p. 1.

global and cosmographical order; rather, the meridian line was the first step in 'perfecting' the country's geography. The map that the *Académie* would produce based on this survey would not merely describe a pre-existing geography; it would actively create that geography based on a new and perfect way of understanding, measuring and controlling space.

The Paris meridian was re-surveyed in the 1730s and the resulting triangulation extended thereafter along the major river valleys of France.[49] By 1744, a national, astronomically accurate grid of relative and absolute distance had been created for most of the country – the so-called 'carte des triangles'.[50] In his quest for money to complete his work, César-François Cassini de Thury (the third in the succession) sold his expertise to noble and royal houses all over Europe and a network of triangulated space, based directly or indirectly on the French model and using the same 1:86,400 scale, gradually extended across central Europe from the 1750s onwards.[51]

By the eve of the French Revolution, with a 180-sheet *Carte de France* based on the post-1744 survey virtually complete, the idealised and absolute geometric space fashioned in France even managed to cross the English Channel as a result of the remarkable collaboration between French surveyors led by Jean-Dominique Cassini (the fourth in the succession) and British surveyors led by William Roy who joined forces to link the Paris and Greenwich observatories by a new line of triangulated space, the template for the mapping of Britain on a European foundation that would begin with the establishment of the Ordnance Survey in 1791.[52]

---

[49] This detailed image of triangulation in the south of France appears in César-François Cassini de Thury, *La méridienne de l'Observatoire royal de Paris* (Paris: Imprimerie Royale, 1744) plate 5. It is reproduced and discussed in Pelletier, Les cartes de Cassini *op. cit.*, p. 89.

[50] Giacomo Maraldi and César-François Cassini de Thury, *Nouvelle carte qui comprend les principaux triangles qui servent de fondement à la description géométrique de la France (Carte des triangles)*, in César-François Cassini de Thury, *La méridienne de l'Observatoire royale de Paris* (Paris: Imprimerie Royale, 1744). A manuscript version of this map is in the Salle des Cartes et Plans, Bibliothèque Nationale de France (Ge.BB.565-A). It is reproduced and discussed in Konvitz, Cartography in France *op. cit.*, p. 17.

[51] One of Cassini's more enthusiastic patrons was the Palatine Elector Karl Theodor whose legacy on the city of Heidelberg, where a shortened version of this chapter was presented as the first Hettner lecture, is still visible everywhere. Cassini, ably assisted by Christian Mayer, the Jesuit professor of mathematics and physics at Heidelberg had apparently impressed Karl Theodor by undertaking a detailed triangulation of a strip of land around the Observatory in the Elector's summer palace at Schwetzingen in 1762. See César-François Cassini de Thury, *Relation des deux voyages faits en Allemagne par ordre du Roi* (Paris: Imprimerie Royale, 1765) pp. 94-95; Adolf Kistner, *Die Pflege der Naturwissenschaften in Mannheim zur Zeit Karl Theodors* (Mannheim: Selbstverlag des Mannheimer Altertumsvereins, 1930) pp. 52-53; and, more generally, Alexander Moutchnik, *Forschung und Lehre in der zweiten Hälfte des 18. Jahrhunderts: Der Naturwissenschaftler und Universitätsprofessor Christian Mayer SJ (1719-1783)* (Augsburg: Dr. Erwin Rauner Verlag, 2006).

[52] The map depicting the triangulation points on either side of the English Channel has been reproduced in several places, including W. A. Seymour (ed.) *A History of the Ordnance Survey* (London: HMSO, 1980); and David Turnbull, 'Cartography and science in early-modern Europe:

The creation of a modern European geometric space continued through the 19th and 20th century facilitated by national and international agencies, the latter exemplified by the *Europäische Gradmessung* established in the 1860s to promote international geodetic mapping.[53] This process was less concerned with the creation of maps as symbolic representations of space and more concerned with the construction of what David Turnbull calls 'knowledge spaces' that were originally national but, from the mid-18th century, increasingly international and pan-European.[54]

Despite the enormous technological changes since the 18th century, the world we live in today is recognisably based on this absolutist geographical imagination; a geometrically ordered world of bounded, controlled and regulated space that is both national, European and now global. The development of the modern idea of Europe, in which all of the narratives I have emphasised have been mobilised, has ultimately generated a particular form of European space. Although no longer limited to Europe itself, of course, this geographical imagination first arose in Europe during the 'long' 18th century and has thus defined European space for longer than anywhere else. Europe has been created through all the narratives I have discussed above but also through this creative geographical process.

Conclusion

In this chapter, I have attempted to deconstruct the modern idea of Europe in terms of five historical narratives. I have also attempted to connect the Europe that has emerged from these narratives with a distinctively European geographical imagination. None of my observations are meant to imply the idea of Europe is empty of meaning or inspiration or that the enormous achievements of the European project since 1945 are anything but wholly desirable and beneficial. But it seems doubtful to me that the idea of Europe outlined here will continue for long into the 21st century. Deconstructing the idea of Europe reveals how complex and contradictory are the foundational myths on which it rests. Acknowledging this is, I believe, the necessary first step towards reconstructing an idea of Europe for the 21st century. Some aspects of the traditional European idea will – and surely must –

---

mapping the construction of knowledge spaces', *Imago Mundi* 48 (1996) pp. 5-24, p. 19. For a general account of this episode, see Sven Widmalm, 'Accuracy, rhetoric, and technology: the Paris-Greenwich triangulation, 1784-88', in Tore Frängsmyr, J. L. Heilbron and Robin E. Rider (eds.) *The Quantifying Spirit in the 18th Century* (Berkeley and Los Angeles: University of California Press, 1990) pp. 179-206.

[53] W. Torge, The International Association of Geodesy 1862 to 1922: from a regional project to an international organization, *Journal of Geodesy* 78 (2005) pp. 558-568

[54] Turnbull, 'Cartography and science in early-modern Europe' *op. cit.*

continue but only if other aspects fade from our collective consciousness. In a justly famous lecture delivered at the Sorbonne in 1882, Ernest Renan posed a deceptively simple question: what is a nation?[55] In his brilliant answer, surely the most eloquent defence of civic patriotism ever formulated, he suggested that nations survive and flourish not because their citizens are able to remember and mobilise a collective heritage. Nations function as meaningful abstractions because these same citizens also collectively forget aspects of their past as well, not in an unthinking way, but as a conscious and deliberate act. If this was an accurate statement about Europe's nations in 1882, and I think it was, it strikes me as an equally compelling statement about Europe as a whole at the beginning of the 21st century.

---

[55] Ernest Renan, 'Qu'est-ce qu'une nation?', in Ernest Renan, *Oeuvres complètes* (Vol. 1, Paris: Calman-Lévy, 1947) pp. 887-906. The essay is translated in Homi Bhabha (ed.) *Nation and Narration* (London: Routledge, 1990) pp. 8-21.

EUROPEAN DREAMING: FRANCE, BRITAIN AND THE NEW EUROPE, C.1914–C.1945

European dreaming: France, Britain and the new Europe, c. 1914 – c. 1945

MICHAEL HEFFERNAN

This essay focuses on the European debate in two countries, France and Britain, during the 1920s and 1930s, with particular reference to the geographies that informed these discussions. As I argued in the introduction, the inter-war period was an especially fruitful era for the European debate as so many of the ideas that would shape the evolution of European institutions after 1945 were first formulated in this earlier period, inspired in part by the economic and political crises which gripped the continent.[1]

This applies especially to the debate in France and Britain. Two radically different European visions took shape in these two countries after 1918. The former was developed early in the 1920s and refined thereafter into a powerful and compelling theory of European economic and political integration that continues to influence French and European debates today. The latter, rooted in earlier 19th century ideas derived from the British imperial experience, was ultimately bypassed and largely forgotten. I want to suggest that the eventual triumph of the French interwar conception of Europe, which was directly influenced by explicitly geographical writings, and the eclipse of the more complex British perspective has had significant consequences for the European project since 1945. A re-examination of these earlier debates, especially those developed in Britain, has considerable relevance for the most recent phase in the European debate.

I do not mean to imply by this that the interwar European debate was in any way limited to France and Britain. The nature and shape of a future Europe was obviously a matter of concern to writers and intellectuals in all parts of Europe and beyond. But France and Britain were the only major western European countries that retained faith in liberal democracy throughout this period, despite the serious threats posed to this form of government in both countries. The ideas of European unity developed in Germany and Italy, in particular, including those devised by geopolitical theorists before and during the authoritarian governments that eventually took power in both

---

[1] See, for example, Carl H. Pegg, *Evolution of the European Idea, 1914-1932* (Chapel Hill: University of North Carolina Press, 1982); Elisabeth du Reau, *L'Idée de l'Europe au XXe. siècle: des myths aux réalités* (Brussels: Éditions Complexe, 1996); and Peter M. R. Stirk, *A History of European Integration since 1914* (London: Pinter, 1996) pp. 18-50. For a direct contrast between Britain and France in the later interwar period, see M. L. Smith, 'Ideas of a new order in France, Britain and the Low Countries in the 1930s', in Peter M. R. Stirk (ed.) *European Unity in Context: The Interwar Period* (London: Pinter, 1989) pp. 149-169.

countries, have been extensively discussed elsewhere. These perspectives are considered in this chapter only in so far as they influenced the French and British discussions that took place.[2]

The analysis draws extensively, though not exclusively, on the writings of professional geographers, not out of disciplinary chauvinism but because the leading geographers of the period enjoyed an unprecedented and probably unique involvement with high level policy formation. The accounts they produced offer some of the most perceptive and revealing commentaries on wider intellectual, political and economic trends.

Geography's revenge: the cartographic anxieties of Versailles Europe

According to the French geographer and historian Jacques Ancel, the Paris peace conferences at the end of World War One represented 'une revanche de la Géographie sur l'Histoire'.[3] This was an apposite remark in more ways than one. At one level, Ancel's remark drew attention to the prominence of geographers and cartographers as expert advisers to political and military leaders during the war and at the peace negotiations. For the first (and probably the last) time, the world's leading politicians had turned to geographers, rather than other social scientists, for solutions to the intractable problems they confronted.[4] But if the events of 1914-1919 demonstrated the utility of geographical knowledge, the outcome gave little comfort to commentators such as Ancel. He was as much an historian as a geographer and his

---

[2] For a discussion of the European debate in German and Italian geopolitics, see discussion and the references cited in Michael Heffernan, *The Meaning of Europe: Geography and Geopolitics* (London: Arnold, 1998) pp. 131-149.

[3] Jacques Ancel, *Peuples et nations des Balkans* (Paris: Armand Colin, 1926) p. 1. The phrase 'cartographic anxieties' is borrowed from the title of the central essay in David Gregory, *Geographical Imaginations* (Oxford: Blackwell, 1994) pp. 70-205.

[4] There is a growing literature on this episode in the history of geography, particularly on the American, French and British experiences. Recent studies, which summarise earlier literature, include Jeremy Crampton, 'The cartographic calculation of space: race mapping and the Balkans at the Paris Peace Conference', *Social and Cultural Geography* 7, 5 (2006) pp. 731-752; Michael Heffernan, 'The spoils of war: the *Société de Géographie de Paris* and the French empire, 1914-1919', in Morag Bell, Robin Butlin and Michael Heffernan (eds.) *Geography and Imperialism 1820-1920* (Manchester: Manchester University Press, 1995) pp. 221-264; Michael Heffernan, 'Geography, cartography and military intelligence: the Royal Geographical Society and the First World War', *Transactions of the Institute of British Geographers* 21, 3 (1996) pp. 504-533; Michael Heffernan, 'Mars and Minerva: centres of geographical calculation in an age of total war', *Erdkunde* 54, 4 (2000) pp. 320-333; Michael Heffernan, 'History, geography and the French national space: the question of Alsace-Lorraine, 1914-1918', *Space and Polity* 5, 1 (2001) pp. 27-48; Gilles Palsky, 'Emmanuel de Martonne and the ethnographical cartography of Central Europe (1917-1920)', *Imago Mundi* 54 (2002) pp. 111-119; and Neil Smith, *American Empire: Roosevelt's Geographer and the Prelude to Globalization* (Berkeley and Los Angeles: University of California Press, 2003) pp. 113-180.

wry observation was intended not as a celebration of geography's triumph but rather as a critique of the new political landscape fashioned by cartographic expediency in 1919. In Ancel's view, the Versailles Treaty was the outcome of a Byzantine process of geographical calculation and compromise between incompatible national demands. Economic, cultural and historical factors had all been downplayed or simply ignored, he believed, in favour of ostensibly neat and simple solutions, 'jeux *avec* frontières' on the European map.[5]

It is worth reminding ourselves about the causes of Ancel's angst. Post-1918 Europe was vastly more complex and divided than it had been before 1914. Over eight million young and productive lives had been lost during the war and economic recovery seemed destined to falter given the many new impediments to intra-European trade created by the Treaty of Versailles. The new Europe had to contend with 35 different currencies and an additional 18,000 kilometres of international border. The circulation of labour resources, relatively easy before 1914, particularly in the Austro-Hungarian empire, now required passports and a mass of new paperwork that kept border guards in gainful employment but had disastrous consequences for economic recovery. In 1912, Europe had accounted for 43% of the world's industrial production and 59% of its trade; by 1923, these figures had fallen to 34% and 50% respectively.[6] The post-1920 upsurge in economic nationalism and tariff competition, which accelerated after the rise of fascism in Italy and National Socialism in Germany, was one of the more predictable outcomes of the new political geography.

The League of Nations, an idea tirelessly promoted by US President Woodrow Wilson and fellow internationalists before and during the peace negotiations and eventually written into the Treaty of Versailles to ensure collective security and hasten the process of economic recovery, was weakened from the outset by the absence of key nations, including the USA itself whose isolationist Senate had rejected the policy of their own President and voted against ratifying the Treaty of Versailles. Germany was missing as well, of course, and would remain outside the League until 1926. Absent too was the USSR which was not admitted until 1934. These latter two states, so pivotal to the European debate, stayed within the League

---

[5] This was substantially the same critique famously developed by John Maynard Keynes. See John Maynard Keynes, *The Economic Consequences of the Peace* (London: Macmillan, 1919). The most famous explicitly geographical commentaries and critiques of the Versailles world order were Halford Mackinder, *Democratic Ideals and Realities: A Study in the Politics of Reconstruction* (London: Constable, 1919); Isaiah Bowman, *The New World: Problems in Political Geography* (New York: World Book Co., 1921); and Jean Brunhes and Camille Vallaux, *La géographie de l'histoire: géographie de la paix et de la guerre sur terre et sur mer* (Paris: Félix Alcan, 1921).

[6] Martin Kitchen, *Europe between the Wars: A Political History* (London: Longman) p. 28 and more generally Derek H. Aldcroft, *Studies in the Interwar European Economy* (Aldershot: Ashgate, 1997).

for only seven and five years respectively, the former withdrawing after the rise of the Nazis, the latter expelled for entering into a bilateral arrangement with them.[7]

The idea that a divided Europe, partly dominated by fascism, was doomed to decline relative to other, more dynamic and economically integrated parts of the world, particularly the USA, was a dominant theme in the European debate through the 1920s, exemplified by the writings of Oswald Spengler and Julien Benda.[8] Paul Valéry summed up the European prospects in 1919 perfectly: 'We hope vaguely, we dread precisely'.[9]

L'Europe et la patrie:
Europe and the French geographical imagination between the wars

These were scarcely conducive circumstances for a major revival in the European debate but, as I have emphasised already, the enthusiasm for imagining new European solutions to national problems tends to flourish at precisely the moments when Europe is most divided and its future most uncertain. In France, the 1920s witnessed a flurry of new publications on the possibility of a more integrated and ultimately united Europe, a prospect increasingly invoked as the only alternative to an otherwise inevitable economic and political decline.

Some of the most perceptive pro-European arguments were advanced by French geographers whose writings were sometimes explicitly experimental, involving the kind of speculative futurology rarely encountered in the discipline before or since.[10] The many inter-war publications of Albert Demangeon were probably the best known and most instructive. As France and the rest of Europe struggled back to normality after the war, Demangeon was confronted with a serious dilemma. As a leading disciple of Paul Vidal de la Blache, the founder of the French school of

---

[7] F. S. Northedge, *The League of Nations: Its Life and Times* (Leicester: Leicester University Press, 1986).

[8] Oswald Spengler, *The Decline of the West* (2 Vols, New York: A. A. Knopf, 1934), originally published in 1918 as *Der Untergang des Abendlandes*; and Julien Benda, *The Treason of the Intellectuals* (New York: Norton, 1928), originally published in 1927 as *La trahison des clercs*.

[9] Paul Valéry, 'On European civilization and the European mind', quoted in Mark Leonard, *Why Europe will Run the 21st Century* (London: Fourth Estate, 2005).

[10] See, for example, Y.-M. Goblet, *Le crépuscule des traités* (Paris: Berger-Levrault, 1934). In this critique of the Versailles political geography, Goblet championed a new experimental political geography as a guide to international policy formation. The economic, political and social implications of different political arrangements should be fully considered, according to an internationally agreed methodology in objective, controlled conditions under the auspices of the League of Nations. For a detailed analysis of this period, see Yannick Muet, *Les géographes et l'Europe: l'idée européenne dans la pensée géopolitique française de 1919 à 1939* (Geneva: Institut européen de l'Université de Genève, 1996).

regional geography in the late 19th century,[11] Demangeon was fully committed to the idea, so tirelessly promoted during the 1914-18 war by his now deceased mentor, that France possessed 'natural' borders, roughly those in existence prior to the Franco-Prussian war of 1870.[12] He therefore fully endorsed the post-war restoration of French authority in the 'lost provinces' of Alsace and Lorraine, the region ceded to Germany in 1871, and had even acted as an adviser to the French delegation negotiating these and other European border adjustments during the peace conferences in 1919. The new geography negotiated at Versailles should be respected by all nations, he believed, and secured through the League of Nations. German and Italian demands to re-negotiate the Versailles Treaty, whether justified in the name of traditional Ratzelian state nationalism or the new revanchism of geopolitical theorists such as Karl Haushofer and Ernesto Massi, had therefore to be resisted at all costs. In Demangeon's view, further alterations to a flawed arrangement would simply exacerbate Europe's difficulties.

And yet Demangeon also recognised that the Europe constructed at Versailles was doomed both economically and politically. Even the long-awaited return of Alsace-Lorraine, France's non-negotiable war aim throughout 1914-18, was tarnished by the growing realisation that the region's separation from the German hinterland with which it had integrated so completely during the preceding four decades, would seriously compromise its continuing industrial development. The Europe of Versailles could not survive, reasoned Demangeon, and the best that could be expected was a slow and inexorable decline as the Old World was progressively usurped by the New World. At worst, Europe would be condemned to another major war within a generation. The possibility of France surviving such a calamity given the terrible losses the country had endured between 1914 and 1918 seemed remote indeed.

Demangeon views on the European dilemma were presented in a remarkable book, published in 1920.[13] His title, *Le déclin de l'Europe*, accurately captured his sense of unease but did not adequately reflect his firm insistence that Europe had a means

---

[11] The literature on Vidal de la Blache and the French regional school is vast, but see Vincent Berdoulay, *La formation de l'école française de géographie* (Paris: Bibliothèque Nationale, 1981); Anne Buttimer, *Society and Milieu in the French Geographic Tradition* (Chicago: University of Chicago Press, 1971); Paul Claval (ed.) *Autour de Vidal de la Blache: la formation de l'école française de géographie* (Paris: CNRS, 1993); and André-Louis Sanguin, *Vidal de la Blache: un génie de la géographie* (Paris: Belin, 1993).

[12] Vidal de la Blache had acted as the Vice-President of the *Comité d'Études*, set up by the French Prime Minister Aristide Briand in early 1917 to develop an intellectually compelling case for the return of Alsace-Lorraine to France and to promote a range of other territorial adjustments in Europe, the Middle East and Africa, all designed to enhance France's power within and beyond Europe. See *Travaux du Comité d'Études: Vol. II: Question Européennes* (Paris: Imprimerie Nationale, 1919) and for a detailed analysis, Heffernan, 'History, geography and the French national space' *op. cit.*

[13] Albert Demangeon, *Le déclin de l'Europe* (Paris: Payot, 1920).

of escape from the Versailles impasse. Demangeon was convinced a new, transnational regional economic geography would eventually emerge within Europe, provided the European nation states avoided the temptations of a 'beggar-thy-neighbour' economic nationalism based on high tariffs on internationally traded commodities. The economic geography of the USA had demonstrated the space-defying power of modern transportation systems, particularly the awesome potential of air transport. Demangeon was convinced these same technologies would create a new Europe where the borders established at Versailles would become increasingly irrelevant. There was no need to re-adjust Europe's internal political geography, concluded Demangeon, for the solution to the continent's geopolitical problems lay in unfettered trade within an integrated European economy. This would require multilateral European political agreement, supported by the League of Nations, to establish a single European market. Once in place, and Demangeon acknowledged that this would be a slow and gradual process, a common European market would inevitably generate some form of European federal government.

Demangeon revised and extended these simple arguments through the 1930s in the light of the global economic depression his earlier analysis had predicted.[14] The rise of National Socialism in Germany gave a renewed impetus to his work, notably through his collaboration with the historian Lucien Febvre, co-founder of the *Annales* school of history.[15] This culminated in a new historical geography of the Rhine that sought to demonstrate that this natural corridor, the backbone of the western European economy, should logically unite rather divide the economic and political spaces to its east and west. The idea that the Rhine might serve as an international border, rather than an economic conduit, was a perverse manifestation of confrontational nationalism.[16]

By the mid-1930s, Demangeon was more convinced than ever that European economic integration was the only way to prevent a future war and the inevitable collapse of European civilisation. He was equally convinced that a united Europe

---

[14] See also Albert Demangeon, 'Les aspects actuels de l'économie internationale', *Annales de Géographie* 38 (1929) pp. 10-25 and pp. 97-112; Albert Demangeon, 'Les aspects nouveaux de l'économie internationale', *Annales de Géographie* 41 (1932) pp. 1-21 and pp. 113-130; Albert Demangeon, 'Les conditions géographiques d'une Union européenne: federation européenne ou ententes régionales', *Annales d'histoire économique et sociale* 4 (1932) pp. 433-451.

[15] The literature on the *Annales* school is extensive, but see Stuart Clark (ed.) *The Annales School: Critical Assessments in History* (4 vols, London: Routledge, 1999) and Peter Burke, *The French Historical Revolution: The Annales School, 1929-1989* (Cambridge: Cambridge University Press, 1990). It is worth emphasising that Febvre's *La terre et l'évolution humaine: introduction géographique de l'histoire* (Paris: La Renaissance du Livre, 1922) was arguably the most powerful post-war re-statement of the concepts of possibilism and *genres de vie* that had shaped Vidal de la Blache's geography.

[16] Albert Demangeon and Lucien Febvre, *Le Rhin: problèmes d'histoire et économie* (Paris: Armand Colin, 1935). See also Peter Schöttler, 'The Rhine as an object of historical controversy in the inter-war years: towards a history of frontier mentalities', *History Workshop Journal* 39 (1995) pp. 1-21.

could only emerge from the French nation state. Other European states had either abandoned the liberal, republican ideals that still shaped French political culture, or were detached from a common European economic project. Just as modern, republican France had emerged from the complexity of its differing regions, so a new Europe would evolve, driven by the same transcendent democratic ideals, from its constituent nation-states. Europe, in Demangeon's vision, was the ecstatic apotheosis of French nationalism.[17]

This was a view of Europe rooted in the Vidalian geographical imagination. The Europe-building process, like the nation-building that had constructed France, would ensure the unity and the diversity of European nation-states. Only in this way would the continent cure itself of racially defined ultra-nationalism and secure forever the ideal of a liberal European patriotism. But like Vidal's invocation of France's elegant hexagonal unity, Demangeon's view of Europe demanded a similarly coherent and bounded sense of European territory. If Europe's internal borders were destined eventually to exert minimal influence on intra-European trade and commerce, Europe's outer limits needed to be defined clearly and precisely, at least in economic terms in relation to other emerging regional confederations. Without external limits, Demangeon argued, Europe would develop neither an integrated economy nor a unified sense of identity.

In a memorable war-time book on Alsace-Lorraine, the region ceded by France to Germany after 1871, Vidal de la Blache had noted that in this frontier zone between two traditional European powers 'le moi prend conscience de lui-même en contact avec le non-moi'.[18] In Demangeon's view, in a united Europe Alsace-Lorraine would no longer be a frontier zone. However, the new Europe Demangeon envisioned would require its own external limits. A European 'moi' would only exist through awareness of a 'non-moi' beyond Europe, the obvious candidates being the emerging continental-scale powers of the USA and the USSR. These two empires, along with Japan, would increasingly look to the Pacific, 'l'océan des pays jeunes', rather than across the Atlantic to Europe.[19]

The European credentials of Great Britain, locked by tradition and conviction into its sprawling global empire, were equally problematic in Demangeon's view. This was a cause for concern and Demangeon sought to develop a persuasive economic and political case for a British retreat from its distant colonies in several publications devoted to Britain and its empire. The British Empire was no longer sustainable in a world of emerging, spatially contiguous pan-regions, argued Demangeon. It had

---

[17] The argument was summed up concisely in the title of a short essay by Lucien Febvre, 'De la France à l'Europe: histoire, psychologies et physiologies nationales', *Annales d'histoire économique et sociale* 4 (1932) pp. 381-384.

[18] Paul Vidal de la Blache, *La France de l'Est* (Paris: Armand Colin, 1917) p. 79.

[19] Demangeon, Le déclin de l'Europe *op. cit.*, p. 92.

become an unnecessary diversion preventing Britain from fulfilling its destiny as a European power.[20]

It might reasonably be argued that there was nothing very original in Demangeon's views. French writers had produced more than their fair share of blueprints for European unity in previous eras, some of which are discussed in chapter one. Many of these programmes, from the Duc de Sully in the mid-17th century to Victor Hugo in the mid-19th century, had insisted on the cultural and political centrality of France within Europe.[21] Demangeon was fully aware of these earlier writings, of course, and frequently invoked them to add the lustre of historical tradition to his pronouncements. However, his work was original in other respects, and significant for my purposes, because it rested on a powerfully articulated geographical imagination that was itself rooted in material economic processes rather than more generalised cultural pronouncements.

Demangeon's European project, which he developed consistently through the interwar period, was widely endorsed, with qualifications and nuances, by other leading French geographers, including the aforementioned Ancel, who engaged more directly than Demangeon with German and Italian geopolitics.[22] The prolific writings of the geographer-jurist André Siegfried, who would eventually serve as a conservative judge at the International Court of Human Rights in The Hague, represented the most complete development of Demangeon's vision.[23]

This was, broadly speaking, the same viewpoint promoted by some of Europe's leading liberal politicians. The faith in a united, federal Europe was most insistently proclaimed by Richard Coudenhove-Kalergi's Pan Europa Union (PEU), launched by the publication of his manifesto, *Pan-Europa*, in Vienna in 1923.[24] Like

---

[20] Albert Demangeon, 'Problèmes britanniques', *Annales de Géographie* 31 (1922) pp. 15-36; Albert Demangeon, *L'Empire britannique: étude de géographie coloniale* (Paris: Armand Colin, 1923); Albert Demangeon, *Les îles britanniques* (Paris: Armand Colin, 1927); Albert Demangeon, 'L'Angleterre, l'Europe et le monde, d'après le livre de Mr Erich Obst', *Annales de Géographie* 37 (1928) pp. 268-270. See also Paul Claval, 'Playing with mirrors: the British Empire according to Albert Demangeon', in Anne Godlewska and Neil Smith (eds.) *Geography and Empire* (Oxford: Blackwell, 1994) pp. 228-243.

[21] See Heffernan, The Meaning of Europe *op. cit*, pp. 8-48.

[22] Jacques Ancel, *Géopolitique* (Paris: Delagrave, 1936); Jacques Ancel, *Manuel géographique de politique européenne* (2 vols, Paris: Delagrave, 1936-45); Jacques Ancel, *Géographie des frontières* (Paris: Gallimard, 1938). On Ancel's conversion from historian to political geographer, see Michael Heffernan, 'Geography, empire and National Revolution in Vichy France', *Political Geography* 24 (2005) pp. 731-758.

[23] André Siegfried, *La crise de l'Europe* (Paris: Calmann-Lévy, 1935). Siegfried devoted much of his academic work to the English speaking world, initiated by writings in the 1920s such as *La crise britannique au XXe. siècle* (Paris: Armand Colin, 1927) and *Les États-Unis d'aujourd'hui* (Paris: Armand Colin, 1927).

[24] Richard Coudenhove-Kalergi, *Pan-Europa* (Vienna: Pan-Europa Verlag, 1923). See also his later *Crusade for Pan-Europe* (New York: Putnam, 1943) and the recent commentary by Daniel C.

Demangeon, Coudenhove-Kalergi felt that a united Europe would need to remain separate economically and politically from the USSR (rejected from the European 'family' on ideological rather than geographical grounds) and Britain (whose dispersed empire was deemed incompatible with full involvement in the European project). The anti-British delineation was not based on an overt anti-imperialism for the united Europe envisioned by Coudenhove-Kalergi would ultimately develop a coordinated colonial presence in Africa, just as the USA was extending its influence in Latin America. In Coudenhove-Kalergi's world view, vast economically integrated confederations of the kind satirised by George Orwell in *1984* would naturally emerge.[25]

By the late 1920s, the PEU had tens of thousands of subscribers, 38 per cent of whom were French. Supporters included some prominent politicians, notably Aristide Briand and Édouard Herriot who had swapped senior French government portfolios throughout the 1920s.[26] Herriot began to develop a political case for a 'United States of Europe' in a series of speeches beginning in 1924 and eventually published a much discussed book with that title in 1930.[27] Briand became Honorary President of the PEU after World War One and as French Foreign Minister, drafted an extraordinary memorandum on 17th May 1930 which he circulated to 26 European governments, including Britain but excluding Russia and Turkey, calling for a new federal European government.[28] The responses to Briand's ambitious but vague memorandum ranged from the openly suspicious to the frankly bewildered (the mandarins in the British Foreign Office managing both these reactions at once) and indicate that the French view of European unity was by no means widely endorsed.[29]

Briand's proposal reveals the extent to which official French policy had been influenced by the prophetic European idealism articulated by academics such as

---

Villanueva, 'Richard von Coudenhove-Kalergi's "Pan-Europa" as the elusive "object of longing"', *Rocky Mountain Review of Language and Literature* 59, 2 (2005) pp. 67-80.

[25] This was, ironically, precisely the same prediction made by German geopolitical theorists, including Karl Haushofer. See Charles-Robert Ageron, 'L'idée de l'Eurafrique et le débat colonial franco-allemand de l'entre-deux-guerres', *Revue d'Histoire Moderne et Contemporaine* 22 (1975) pp. 446-475; and John O'Loughlin and Herman van der Wusten, 'The political geography of pan-regions', *Geographical Review* 80, 1 (1990) pp. 1-20.

[26] Pegg, Evolution of the European Idea *op. cit.*, p. 51.

[27] Édouard Herriot, *The United States of Europe* (New York: Viking Press, 1930).

[28] Cornelia Navari, The origins of the Briand plan, in Andrea Bosco (ed.) *The Federal Idea: Vol. 1 – The History of Federalism from the Enlightenment to 1945* (London: Lothian Foundation Press, 1991) pp. 210-235.

[29] Robert Boyce, 'Britain's first 'no' to Europe', *European Studies Review* 10 (1980) pp. 17-45; Philip J. Morgan, '"A vague and puzzling idealism…": plans for European unity in the era of the modern state', in Wintle, Culture and Identity in Europe *op. cit.*, pp. 33-51; Ralph White, 'Cordial caution: the British response to the French proposal for European Federal Union of 1930', in Bosco, The Federal Idea *op. cit.*, pp. 236-262.

Demangeon. The plan also represented the 20th century climax of the long-standing belief that France and Europe ultimately rest on the same intellectual and ideological foundations; that it is possible and necessary to hold these two geopolitical concepts together as mutually reinforcing rather than mutually exclusive projects; that the more 'Europe' there is, the more 'France' there will inevitably be; and that the creation of a federal, united Europe therefore represents the culmination of the French national project.

This was a stirring idea for many French citizens, to be sure, though the geopolitical limits on which a French Europe rested were not universally accepted. In a fascinating essay published in 1926, the historian-geographer Henri Hauser launched a vigorous critique of the pan-European project of Coudenhove-Kalergi and his supporters, including Demangeon, insisting that both Britain and Russia had every right to assert their European culture and civilisation. Britain, in particular, had done more than any other state to spread European values of liberty and democracy around the world. Excluding Britain from a European federation because of its global presence was based on an absurd 'déterminisme géographique' which defined Europe as a closed space. A sealed off Europe would not solve the problems of the old nation-states, notably the tendency towards economic nationalism, but would merely shift these difficulties to a larger scale. This was 'une chimère dangereuse puisque si de cette Europe on exclut l'Angleterre, on coupe le plus solide des cables qui unissent nos vieilles nations aux jeunes communautés européennes d'outre-mer'.[30]

Civitas Dei:
Europe and the British geographical imagination between the wars

Given the tendency of continental theorists to exclude Britain from federal schemes, what, if anything did British intellectuals (geographers included) contribute to the European debate in this period? Pessimism about Europe's future was as pronounced in Britain as it was in France, as was the sense of dismay that the re-organisation of Europe seemed destined to hasten Europe's post-war demise.[31] Halford Mackinder's *Democratic Ideals and Realities*, hastily prepared at the end of the war as a rebuttal to Wilsonian idealism and a resolutely geographical critique of those

---

[30] Henri Hauser, 'Qu'est-ce que l'Europe?' *Le Monde Nouveau: Revue Mensuelle Internationale* 6-7 (1926) pp. 681-688, quotation on p. 685.

[31] British academics had been no less involved than their French counterparts in the campaign to bring about this re-organisation, especially in respect of the Austro-Hungarian Empire where the historian R. W. Seton-Watson and his journal *The New Europe* were especially influential. See Hugh Seton-Watson and Christopher Seton-Watson, *The Making of a New Europe: R. W. Seton-Watson and the Last Years of Austria-Hungary* (Seattle: University of Washington Press, 1981).

who placed undue faith in the League of Nations, predicted a bleak European future in precisely these terms. In Mackinder's view, the rise of extra-European, land-based regional confederations would lead to the steady eclipse of European hegemony, an analysis that culminated with his uncannily prophetic judgement that Europe would eventually divide into two culturally and ideologically distinct zones, one orientated to the west, the other to the east.[32]

Not everyone shared this gloomy assessment. Many British commentators enthusiastically endorsed the federal option outlined by Demangeon and others, without accepting either the underlying Franco-centric logic or the insistence that Britain was faced with a stark choice between Europe and the Empire. Indeed, a radically different vision of an economically and politically integrated Europe can be detected in Britain before and after World War One which echoed the critique of the orthodox French position developed by Henri Hauser above. This would eventually culminate in a remarkable outpouring of British writings on the possibility of a federal Europe during World War Two. In drawing attention to this literature, I want to stress the continuity in British thinking from early 20th century debates about the need to reform and re-organise the British Empire along federal lines through to the British proposals developed before and during World War Two for a federal Europe based initially on a formal union of Britain and France.

Two overlapping movements were central to these debates: the Round Table, which agitated for imperial reform before and after World War One, and the Federal Union, which advocated a new European union during World War Two. The Round Table was a loose association of English imperial reformists of Tory inclination inspired, in one way or another, by the global imperial ambitions of Cecil Rhodes.[33]

---

[32] Mackinder, Democratic Ideals and Realities *op. cit*. Mackinder's analysis drew heavily on his much-quoted 1904 essay (Halford J. Mackinder, 'The geographical pivot of history', *Geographical Journal* 23 (1904) pp. 421-442) the implications of which are still be debated today. See, for example, the theme issue of the *Geographical Journal* 170, 4 (2004) as well as Brian Blouet (ed.) *Global Geostrategy: Mackinder and the Defence of the West* (Abingdon: Frank Cass, 2005).

[33] Andrea Bosco and A. May (eds.) *The Round Table, the Empire/Commonwealth, and British Foreign Policy* (London: Lothian Foundation Press, 1997) and John Kendle, *The Round Table Movement and Imperial Reform* (Toronto: University of Toronto Press, 1975). The Round Table is often discussed in decidedly conspiratorial terms, fuelled by the obvious Arthurian connotations of its name. The fact that most members were civil servants, diplomats, academics and journalists rather than elected politicians meant that whatever influence they wielded was deployed 'behind the scenes', the preferred location for conspiracy seekers. The main source of Round Table conspiracies was Carroll Quigley, a historian at the Edmund A. Walsh School of Foreign Service at Georgetown University who received a surprisingly positive endorsement from Bill Clinton in his 1992 speech accepting the Democratic nomination for the US Presidency. Quigley's *The Anglo-American Establishment from Rhodes to Cliveden* (New York: Books in Focus, 1981) originally written in 1949 but only published four years after the author's death in 1977, argues that the British Round Table was the foundation of an 'international Anglophile network' which Quigley alleged was working secretly for a single global government for much of the 20th century, initially in Britain and

The more direct influence, however, particularly after the death of Rhodes in 1902, was Lord Milner. Most members of the Round Table had previously been recruited as young men to work as civil servants in South Africa during Milner's period as High Commissioner in the colony from 1897 to 1905. The members of Milner's 'kindergarten', as these young men were called, included John Buchan (who later found fame as the gung-ho adventure novelist), Robert Henry Brand (later Lord Brand, a wealthy businessman), Geoffrey Dawson (later editor of *The Times*) and Fabian Ware (who subsequently directed the Imperial War Graves Commission). Other 'fellow travellers' not directly involved in Milner's civil service but who spent time in South Africa and joined the informal debating club he encouraged included Edward Wood (later Lord Halifax, the British Foreign Secretary in the late 1930s) and Leo Amery (subsequently a prominent Conservative MP and writer). The two most significant members of the 'kindergarten' for my purposes were Lionel Curtis and Philip Kerr, for they were also prominently involved in the Federal Union. Nearly all the members of Milner's 'kindergarten' had been educated at Oxford, with an unusually high proportion being associated with New College. Almost half of all Round Table members were subsequently elected to Fellowships at All Souls College, Oxford.[34]

Britain's rather dismal showing in the Boer War convinced Milner and his young followers that the British Empire was unsustainable economically and geopolitically and in need of radical overhaul. And yet without some version of its Empire, British influence in the world would rapidly be eclipsed. The only solution, they believed, was a genuine 'imperial federation', a Commonwealth of Nations each independent but committed to a transcendent form of British liberal, democratic government in which a constitutional monarchy would be retained. This would necessitate the wholesale transfer of defence, foreign and colonial policies from Westminster to a new imperial parliament, which would meet in different places as required, made up

---

eventually in both Britain and the USA. The fact that there was nothing remotely secret about these ambitions did not stop Quigley from developing a fascinating, though unlikely conspiracy theory, supposedly based on secret papers to which he claimed to have been given privileged access for two years in the early 1960s. Quigley claimed these documents proved the existence of a shadowy Anglo-American establishment which controlled the main political parties in the USA and the UK and arranged elections as staged events to satisfy an entirely notional commitment to democracy. The wonderfully strange American fantasy writer John Crowley also uses the idea of a Rhodes-Milner 'secret society' that has been secretly controlling the world since the early 20th century as the basis of his fascinating novella about time travel, *Great Work of Time* (New York: Bantam Press, 1989).

[34] See Richard Symonds, *Oxford and Empire: The Last Lost Cause* (Oxford: Clarendon Press, 1986) and, more specifically, Walter Nimock, *Milner's Young Men: The 'Kindergarten' in Edwardian Imperial Politics* (Durham, NH: Duke University Press, 1968); Saul Dubow, 'Colonial nationalism, the Milner kindergarten and the rise of "South Africanism", 1902-1910', *History Workshop Journal* 43 (1997) pp. 53-86.

of representatives from all the self-governing parts of the new Empire. Never again would British troops have to fight a costly war in far-flung colonies in a futile attempt to maintain the Empire by force.

The Milner circle eventually established a quarterly periodical, published by Macmillan, bearing the title *The Round Table*. The first edition appeared in 1910 and was subtitled 'A Quarterly Review of the Politics of the British Empire'. It included articles from and about different parts of the Empire and promised informed analysis of all colonial and imperial affairs and international relations more generally. Early issues contained articles on Anglo-German rivalry, Japanese ambitions in East Asia, the foreign policy of the United States, and trends in contemporary Islam. All contributions were anonymous, a deliberate policy to indicate the movement's collective commitment to the same general viewpoint. No details were provided on the editor or the editorial board, though we know from other sources that the journal was edited by Philip Kerr until 1917 and thereafter by Reginald Coupland until 1919 (and again between 1939 and 1941), Lionel Curtis from 1919 to 1921, John Dove from 1921 to 1934, Henry V. Hodson from 1934 to 1939, and finally Geoffrey Dawson from 1941 to 1944. The journal continues today, sub-titled the 'Commonwealth Journal of International Affairs', and bills itself as 'the oldest international affairs journal' in the world.[35]

Alongside the journal, the Milner group published dozens of pamphlets and books, sometimes under a collective moniker. Lionel Curtis, who resigned from his post in the Transvaal civil service in 1907 to devote himself full-time to the campaign to create a federal South Africa within a federated British Empire, was probably the most prolific Round Table author.[36] During World War One, Curtis and Kerr wrote a series of essays and books arguing that the British Empire should immediately be transformed into a Commonwealth of equal nations based on a single, supra-national federal parliament and a common citizenship.[37] These proposals went far beyond mere advocacy of the liberal imperial reforms others advocated to stave off a future catastrophic collapse in imperial authority. Curtis and Kerr envisaged a rapid shift from the constitutionally vague Empire into a more clearly defined federal Commonwealth that would ultimately evolve into a world government: 'For England

---

[35] http://www.moot.org.uk

[36] On Curtis, see Daniel Gorman, 'Lionel Curtis, imperial citizenship, and the quest for unity', *The Historian* 66, 1 (2004) pp. 67-90; Deborah Lavin, 'Lionel Curtis and the idea of Commonwealth', in Frederick Madden and David Fieldhouse (eds.) *Oxford and the Idea of Commonwealth: Essays Presented to Sir Edgar Williams* (London: Croom Helm, 1982) pp. 46-65; and Deborah Lavin, *From Empire to International Commonwealth: A Biography of Lionel Curtis* (Oxford: Clarendon Press, 1995).

[37] See Lionel Curtis, *The Problem of the Commonwealth* (London: Macmillan, 1915); Lionel Curtis (ed.) *The Commonwealth of Nations: An Inquiry into the Nature of Citizenship in the British Empire, and into the Mutual Relations of Several Communities Thereof* (London: Macmillan, 1916); Philip Kerr, *Commonwealth and Empire* (London: Macmillan, 1916).

the change is indeed a great one', wrote Curtis, 'Can she face it? Can she bear to lose her life, as she knows it, to find it in a Commonwealth, wide as the world itself, a life greater and nobler than before? Will she fail at this second and last crisis of her fate, as she failed at the first, like Athens and Prussia, forsaking freedom for power, thinking the shadow more real than the light, and esteeming the muckrake more than the crown?'[38]

World War One reinforced the Round Table's convictions about the urgent need for self-government within a re-organised Commonwealth, notably in connection with Ireland and India. The journal's sub-title reflected this shift. From 1919, it was billed as 'A Quarterly Review of the Politics of the British Commonwealth'. Curtis and Kerr were by now the key figures in the movement, their influence secured by the prominent role they had played at the Paris peace conferences in 1919, the former as an adviser on colonial affairs, the latter as Private Secretary to Lloyd George from 1917 to 1921. Curtis famously drafted a memo while in Paris in 1919 arguing for a new, permanent British-backed institution to foster debate and allow sensitive international affairs to be discussed under agreed rules of confidentiality, an idea that culminated with the creation in 1926 of the Royal Institute of International Affairs at Chatham House in London. Curtis was also the principal architect of the so-called 'dyarchy' established under the 1919 Government of India Act as a kind of half-way house to self-government.[39] He also acted as chief adviser on Irish affairs in the Colonial Office from 1921 to 1924 during the difficult transition to independence.[40]

By the mid-1920s, both Kerr and Curtis had developed pronounced pacifist inclinations, the latter informed by strong religious convictions.[41] Curtis subsequently expanded his arguments into a sweeping three-volume philosophical history of the world, *Civitas Dei*, which bears comparison with the great global histories of the period by Oswald Spengler, Arnold Toynbee and H. G. Wells.[42] Beginning with a critical commentary on St. Augustine's *Civitate Dei*, Curtis argued that world government evolving from an overlapping series of regional confederations was the only viable alternative to a general collapse of order and civilisation. Of all the modern powers, Britain was uniquely placed to bring about a global government. It

---

[38] Curtis, The Problem of the Commonwealth *op. cit.*, p. 104.

[39] Lionel Curtis, *Papers Relating to the Application of the Principle of Dyarchy to the Government of India* (Oxford: Clarendon Press, 1920).

[40] Anon., Ireland, *The Round Table* 11 (1921) 345-349; reprinted in Lionel Curtis, *Ireland* (Belfast: Belfast Historical Society, 2002).

[41] Philip Kerr and Lionel Curtis, *The Prevention of War* (New Haven: Yale University Press, 1924).

[42] Lionel Curtis, *Civitas Dei* (3 vols, London: Macmillan, 1934-7). An abridged 1938 edition, published in a single volume, carried the revealing sub-title *The Commonwealth of God*. For Kerr's thinking on the avoidance of war, see Philip Kerr, *The Ending of Armageddon* (London: Macmillan, 1935).

had the longest tradition of democracy and had bequeathed this fragile but noble political system to other countries, notably the USA. Britain's long experience of empire provided the obvious foundations on which a new global government might emerge. Unless it embraced this destiny, Britain was doomed to an inexorable and perhaps dramatic fall.

The Round Table continued to advocate closer political and economic co-operation between Britain and the now fully self-governing Dominion governments in Canada, Australia, New Zealand and South Africa through the 1920s and 1930s while also campaigning for ever closer alliance between the Commonwealth and the USA. The objective was a formal constitutional alliance, based on common citizenship, between the English-speaking peoples in all existing and former British colonies, including the Americas.[43] By the early 1930s, the Round Table's enthusiasm for new federations extended to the idea of a united Europe, based on a formal constitutional union between Britain and France with which other European states could subsequently merge.[44] This distinctively British enthusiasm for a United States of Europe was advocated in a range of successful pamphlets and books, including a widely read volume by the prominent diplomat and historian Sir Arthur Salter which was a sustained and sympathetic engagement with Herriot, Briand and other continental European federalists.[45]

As this implies, the Round Table felt there was no need for Britain to choose between Empire and new political alliances across the Atlantic with the USA and with a new continental federation in Europe. These federal alliances could, and should, be realised at once. Indeed, it was only by creating a network of overlapping federations that Britain's unique parliamentary democracy could survive in the 20th century. From the Round Table's perspective, the lingering 'splendid isolation' of the Victorian imperial age would be destroying the very thing old-style conservatives claimed to cherish most – the British way of life. Ultimately, Britain could only exist at a global level and within the context of a global government.

The outbreak of war in 1939 was a testing time for the Round Table, as several members were condemned for having advocated a policy of appeasement towards

---

[43] Anon., 'The Commonwealth and the world', *The Round Table* 25 (1934-5) 217-233. For a positive American reaction, see Clarence K. Streit, *Union Now with Britain* (London: Jonathan Cape, 1941).

[44] See, as examples, Anon., 'The malady of Europe', *The Round Table* 12 (1922) pp. 751-781; Anon., 'The problem of Europe', *The Round Table* 14 (1923-4) pp. 13-26; Anon., 'Europe, the Covenant and the Protocol', *The Round Table* 15 (1924-5) pp. 219-241; Anon., 'Europe at the crossroads', *The Round Table* 16 (1925-6) pp. 476-501; Anon., 'The United States of Europe', *The Round Table* 20 (1929-30) pp. 79-99; Anon., 'Where is Europe going?', *The Round Table* 21 (1930-1) pp. 1-16; and Anon., 'Great Britain and Europe', *The Round Table* 26 (1935-6) pp. 17-29.

[45] Arthur Salter, *The United States of Europe and other Papers* (London: G. Allen & Unwin, 1933). Salter was elected to what is now known as the Gladstone Chair of Government at the University of Oxford in 1934 and subsequently served as MP for the University.

Nazi Germany during the late 1930s. The journal remained in circulation, however, and continued the call for a post-war federal Europe, though with no mention of a future German role.[46] These arguments developed in a more systematic fashion by a new and more left-wing organisation, the Federal Union, which had been established in the wake of the Munich crisis in September 1938 by journalists Charles Kimber and Derek Rawnsley with the active support of several Round Table members, including Kerr and Curtis. An initial Federal Union pamphlet, printed in 1939 and written by Kimber, Rawnsley and another journalist, Patrick Ransome, called for the immediate union of Britain, France and all other democratic European countries committed to resisting Nazi Germany and its allies.

By 1940, the Federal Union had established a Research Institute at University College Oxford where the Master, William Beveridge, was an enthusiastic supporter. It had also created over 200 branches in towns and cities around the city.[47] More than 12,000 supporters received the organisation's newsletter, the *Federal Union News*, and its regular pamphlets, collectively known as the 'Federal Tracts'. Most were written by the organisation's 'panel of advisers' which included both Curtis and Kerr.[48] The latter, by now Lord Lothian and newly appointed as Britain's Ambassador to the USA, agreed that his 1935 Round Table pamphlet *The Ending of Armageddon* could be re-printed and circulated as a Federal Union tract, alongside a series of new, bluntly titled pamphlets by the ever-willing Curtis.[49] The most widely

---

[46] Anon., 'Union: oceanic or continental', *The Round Table* 29 (1938-9) pp. 733-744; Anon., 'World trade and the future', *The Round Table* 29 (1938-9) pp. 782-797; Anon., 'War and peace', *The Round Table* 30 (1939-40) pp. 5-26; Anon., 'Europe on the eve', *The Round Table* 33 (1942-3) pp. 204-209; Anon., 'Reflections on the new Europe', *The Round Table* 34 (1943-4) pp. 199-203; and Anon., 'Shaping the new Europe', *The Round Table* 35 (1944-5) pp. 117-121.

[47] Richard Mayne, John Pinder and John Roberts, *The Federal Union: The Pioneers* (London: Macmillan, 1990). For Beveridge's own writings, see his *Peace by Federation* (Oxford: Oxford University Press/Federal Union, 1940). The Federal Union archives, including all its pamphlets, are housed at the London School of Economics.

[48] Also involved were Lionel Robbins (the prominent economist), Ronald 'Kim' Mackay (an Australian-born writer and later a Labour MP), Sir Richard Acland (a former Liberal who moved progressively to the left through the 1930s having established a short-lived Common Wealth Party with the writer J. B. Priestley during World War I and was subsequently a pioneering activist in the early Campaign for Nuclear Disarmament), Ivor Jennings (a leading constitutional lawyer and reforming educationalist in India and Ceylon who later became Master of Trinity Hall, Cambridge), Drummond Shiels (a Labour MP and Undersecretary of State for the Colonies in Ramsey Macdonald's 1929 government), Henry Usborne (another Labour MP and a tireless advocate of world government through the One World Trust), Barbara Wootton (the University of London sociologist), H. N. Brailsford (the socialist writer and journalist), C. E. M. Joad (the socialist philosopher and writer), Konni Zilliacus (the pacifist Labour MP and journalist), Henry Wickham-Stead (a former editor of *The Times*) and Kingsley Martin (the editor of *The Spectator*).

[49] Lord Lothian, *The Ending of Armageddon* (Oxford: Oxford University Press/Federal Union, 1940); Lionel Curtis, *Decision* (Oxford: Oxford University Press/Federal Union, 1941); Lionel Curtis, *Action* (Oxford: Oxford University Press/Federal Union, 1942); Lionel Curtis, *Decision and Action*

read Federal Union tracts were, however, W. B. Curry's *The Case for Federal Union* and Kim Mackay's *Federal Europe* which each sold well over 100,000 copies.[50] According to one historian, the flood of war-time British writing on the possibilities of European federal union was a truly unprecedented achievement: 'Despite the flow of material on the subject of European integration in the post-war years, it is doubtful whether such an impressive combination of quality and quantity has been produced in such a short period in any country since'.[51]

In contrast to their colleagues in France, British geographers made only minor contributions to the British federal debate, with the notable exception of C. B. Fawcett who wrote several essays and books before and during World War Two in terms that echoed Round Table and Federal Union arguments. In one essay, Fawcett argued that 'the world is now the only possible final unit for the political and economic organization of mankind'. A World Commonwealth would need to emerge from what he called the European 'focal area' where 'already converge the homelands of three of the leading peoples – British, French, and Germans – as well as those of some of the more important smaller nations'. A united Europe was not an end in itself, however, but only a necessary first step towards a global federation which the former imperial powers, especially Britain, were best placed to bring about: 'no practicable union of European peoples can be limited to that continent', insisted Fawcett for 'Europe, as a major world region, is so intimately related to many other parts of the world that it cannot be isolated without complete disaster to its present economic and cultural development. There is no hope, even for Europe itself, in a United States of Europe limited to Europe. Here isolationism is suicide'.[52]

British inter-war federalism can easily be dismissed as naïve and idealistic, the sort of musing encouraged by Oxford's 'dreaming spires'. But it is worth emphasising that the Round Table had a clear and definite impact on the transition from Empire to

---

(Oxford: Oxford University Press/Federal Union, 1942). On Lothian's role in the USA, see David Reynolds, 'Lord Lothian and Anglo-American relations, 1939-1940', *Transactions, American Philosophical Society* 73 (1983) Part I.

[50] W. B. Curry, *The Case for Federal Union* (Harmondsworth: Penguin, 1939); Ronald 'Kim' Mackay, *Federal Europe, being the case for European Federation together with a Draft Constitution of a United States of Europe* (London: M. Joseph, 1940). See also H. N. Brailsford, *The Federal Idea* (London: Federal Union, 1940); Ivor W. Jennings, *A Federation of Western Europe* (Cambridge: Cambridge University Press, 1940); Frances L. Josephy, *Europe: The Key to Peace* (London: Macmillan, 1944); F. A. Ridley and B. Edwards, *The United Socialist States of Europe* (London: New Left Books, 1944); John Strachey, *Federalism or Socialism?* (London: New Left Books, 1940).

[51] John Pinder, The Federal Union, 1939-41, in Walter Lipgens (ed.) *Documents on the History of European Integration: Vol. II – Plans for European Union in Great Britain and in Exile, 1939-1945* (Berlin: de Gruyter for the European University Institute, Florence, 1986) pp. 26-34, quotation on p. 26.

[52] Charles B. Fawcett, *The Bases of a World Commonwealth* (London: C. A. Watts, 1941), quotations on pp. 1, 45 and 64. See also Charles B. Fawcett, 'Some geographical factors in world unity', *New Commonwealth Quarterly* 6 (1940) pp. 95-101.

Commonwealth, though the modern Commonwealth admittedly bears little comparison with the ambitious programmes proposed by Curtis, Kerr and their colleagues.[53] The Federal Union also provided the intellectual context that facilitated and later justified Winston Churchill's famous proposal to establish 'an indissoluble' Anglo-French union in the exceptional circumstances of June 1940. Had Churchill's offer been accepted, however, France and Britain would have entered the darkest era of their history not as two separate nations 'but one Franco-British Union... with joint organs of defence, foreign, financial and economic policies. Every citizen of France will enjoy immediately citizenship of Great Britain; every British subject will become a citizen of France'.[54]

Conclusion

Given the significance of French and British interwar debates about European federalism, one might reasonably expect that the versions of Europe developed in each country would have continued to influence national policies and the European debate more generally after 1945. In the event, only the French version survived into the post-war era and has indeed determined French foreign policy and much of the European debate ever since. Britain's early interest in a federal Europe seemed to fade rapidly after 1945 and has been almost entirely effaced from popular memory. The explanation for these divergent paths lies in the very different experiences of the two countries during World War Two. In France, defeat and occupation confirmed the views expressed by inter-war European federalists who had predicted that France's prospects as an isolated liberal and democratic state in a divided Europe were bleak indeed. *Les années noires* reinforced the conviction that France's only option was to re-invent itself at the European scale. In Britain, World War Two produced an entirely different reaction and established the single most important facet of the British national mythology – the familiar narrative of Britain 'standing alone' against overwhelming odds, pitting itself against a European continent united by force and eventually emerging in triumphant victory. The idea that post-war Britain might seek economic and political salvation in a federal Europe seemed inconceivable in the wake of this experience. The intriguing British interwar debates that sought to define the terms on which this merger might take place were quickly forgotten.

---

[53] Nicholas Mansergh, *The Commonwealth and the Nations: Studies in British Commonwealth Relations* (London: Royal Institute of International Affairs, 1948); Nicholas Mansergh, *The Commonwealth Experience* (London: Weidenfeld and Nicolson, 1969).

[54] Avi Schlaim, 'Prelude to downfall: the British offer of union to France, June 1940', *Journal of Contemporary History* 9 (1974) pp. 27-63.

It is worth re-visiting these earlier debates, however, because they de-stabilise the meta-narratives that have defined what it means to be French, British and European in the post-war era. They also provide, in the British case especially, an unexpected reservoir of intriguing ideas of direct relevance to Europe's present conditions. The story of French inter-war federalism suggests that although there is undoubtedly a very long French tradition of conceptualising Europe as the climax of French nationalism, the main contours of this argument were formulated only after World War One when the tragic irony of the country's position became clear. The French view of Europe, a view that still shapes official policy to this day, was a product of the interwar period and reflected the widespread recognition that France was unlikely to survive as a traditional nation-state in the Europe created at Versailles. The experience of World War Two confirmed this analysis.

The story of British inter-war federalism sits even more uncomfortably within the accepted narratives. The conventional wisdom, both on the continent of Europe and in Britain itself, suggests that British political culture has never been able to accommodate the idea of supra-national governmental authority. At least two reasons have been advanced to explain this apparent fact. First, as an existing union of different nations, British political life apparently finds it difficult to find room for an additional European scale of authority and almost impossible to accommodate a European identity. Second, Britain's 'special' relationship with the non-European world, particularly the English-speaking former colonies and the USA, supposedly weakens its potential bonds with European allies. In other words, the idea of Europe and the idea of Britain appear to be mutually exclusive rather than mutually reinforcing concepts. And yet, in the federalist debate of the interwar period, these very same national characteristics were interpreted to make precisely the opposite argument. Britain's experience as an outward looking, multi-national and reforming colonial power with close links to the wider English-speaking world meant that it had a natural affinity to develop new alliances within a federal Europe. From this perspective, Britain should be the natural leader of a new European federation rather than one of its constituting 'others'.

French and British views of European federation between the wars were radically different, though both perspectives were championed with comparable energy and conviction by persuasive and influential advocates in academia, politics and journalism. These perspectives rested on fundamentally different geographical imaginations. In France, a united, federal Europe was seen as a logical extension of the archetypical European nation-state – France itself. As the culmination of the French national project, Europe had therefore to rest on the same spatial mythology that had defined France. A Europe fashioned in the image of France needed its own 'limites naturelles'. In Britain, by contrast, the European idea emerged from a national and imperial geographical imagination in which space was conceived in terms of long-distance, often global networks and flows. This was not a bounded, supra-national territory but a transcendent, flexible and porous region. For British federalists, a united Europe, in which Britain would play a central role, did not require spatial limits, natural or otherwise, for such an entity would always look outwards and be defined by its connections with emerging federations elsewhere in the world with which it might ultimately converge. The British perspective, though largely overlooked for the past half century, is probably a more interesting starting point for a new European political culture in the 21st century.

THE NEW COSMOPOLITANISM: EUROPEAN GEOGRAPHIES FOR THE 21ST CENTURY

The new cosmopolitanism:
European geographies for the 21st century

MICHAEL HEFFERNAN

This essay considers aspects of the European debate in the past few decades, with a particular emphasis on the last ten years. The opening three sections briefly review the debate from the 1970s to the 1990s. The final three sections adopt a more speculative tone and draw on a body of literature generated in the last decade that has sought to sketch out the contours of a new European political culture, and perhaps even a new European political geography, for the 21st century.

As I argued in the prologue, although inter-governmental institutions and agencies designed to facilitate European integration were finally established after 1945, their creation was motivated by a simple and compelling economic logic that left precious little room for wider discussion about the essential meaning of Europe in the post-war era. The objective was as simple as it was urgent – to ensure the rapid recovery of the war-ravaged European economies so they might meet the urgent material needs of their populations. No European state was capable of achieving this on its own according to the rules that had governed the region's trade prior to the war. An enhanced measure of economic unity, initially focused on the key commodities of coal, iron and steel, was therefore the only conceivable option available to the western European nation-states.[1]

The political consequences of economic unity were momentous, of course, but most Europeans seemed reasonably comfortable with the idea that 'ever closer union' would eventually create a federal European Union. Those harbouring reservations in the six original European Economic Community (EEC) nations, were generally willing to shelve their concerns while the process retained its essentially economic rationale, as it did until the 1970s. After all, the EEC was helping to ensure impressive growth rates and low levels of unemployment in most member states throughout the three decades from the end of World War Two to the mid-1970s, the period the French call, somewhat nostalgically, 'les trentes glorieuses'.[2] For the eminently practical technocrats who constructed the original EEC, a wide-ranging debate about the core values that might shape a new European political culture

---

[1] John Gillingham, *Coal, Steel, and the Rebirth of Europe, 1945-1955: The Germans and French from Ruhr Conflict to Economic Community* (Cambridge: Cambridge University Press, 1991); Alan S. Milward, *The Reconstruction of Western Europe, 1945-1951* (London: Methuen, 1984); Peter M. R. Stirk and David Willis (eds.) *Shaping Postwar Europe: European Unity and Disunity 1945-1957* (London: Pinter, 1991).

[2] The term, familiar to every French school pupil, is often attributed to Jean Fourastié, *Les trentes glorieuses, ou la revolution invisible de 1945 à 1975* (Paris: Fayard, 1979).

seemed likely to create division rather unity. Who could possibly wish further discussion about the more unappealing programmes advanced by pan-European theorists during the inter-war period?

This does not imply that western European economic integration after 1945 was devoid of ideological motivations, of course, for the entire process was defined by the simple geopolitical realities of the Cold War and the division of Europe at the end of World War Two. The massive injection of US capital under the Marshall Plan had been more or less openly designed to shore up western Europe's fragile, war-damaged economies and thus preserve democracy from the threat of domestic communist take-over.[3] This political objective was entirely consistent with the European programme for economic integration, of course, but was regarded more as a background ideological assumption rather than a matter for serious dispute. The anti-communism underlying the process of economic integration did not provoke any significant renewed debate about the scope and meaning of Europe because the region's global hegemony had ended and there seemed little point discussing its wider meaning in the discredited terms of the past. The 'old' continent that had attracted such grandiose cultural and political speculation across the centuries was now divided between, and controlled by, two non-European superpowers, the USA and USSR. These new empires had assumed the global interests and ambitions of the European colonial powers.

The Cold War division of Europe facilitated the twin and parallel processes of military and economic integration on either side of this divide but it also placed severe limits on the terms within which the European debate could be conducted. In Soviet-dominated Eastern Europe, and within the Communist Parties in western Europe, the very term 'Europe' was studiously avoided and used only in the narrowest geographical sense or in order to attack the process of western European economic integration and the entrenchment in the region of American economic and military power. In the west, where the USA was now the principal military presence, the idea of Europe was couched entirely in Atlanticist terms. This was a region defined by the NATO security ideal of a unified Atlantic arena, an idea that owed far more to American (and to some extent British) geopolitics than anything previously articulated in Europe.[4] The sole achievement of post-war European integration was to add an economic narrative to this security discourse.

---

[3] See, for recent commentaries, John Agnew and J. Nicholas Entrikin (eds.) *The Marshall Plan: Model and Metaphor* (London: Routledge, 2004); Martin Schain (ed.) *The Marshall Plan: Fifty Years After* (London: Palgrave, 2001).

[4] Francis H. Heller and John R. Gillingham (eds.) *NATO: The Founding of the Atlantic Alliance and the Integration of Europe* (New York: St. Martin's Press, 1992); Francis H. Heller and John R. Gillingham (eds.) *The United States and the Integration of Europe: Legacies of the Postwar Era* (New York: St. Martin's Press, 1996); Stanley R. Sloan, *NATO, the European Union, and the Atlantic Community: The Transatlantic Bargain Challenged* (2nd ed., Lanham, MD: Rowman and Littlefield, 2005).

The Atlantic European vision was expressed more powerfully by Americans rather than Europeans, and none were more eloquent than President John F. Kennedy. His address in the shadow of the Berlin Wall is probably the most widely quoted speech about Europe's future but the remarks he made on the preceding day, 25th June 1963, in Frankfurt's Paulskirche were in many respects more revealing for they delineate the Atlantic vision while also pointing optimistically towards an eventual political union between the US and a new European Union. While cautioning that a single 'Atlantic Community will not soon become a single overarching superstate', Kennedy insisted that 'practical steps towards stronger common purpose are well within our means. As we widen our common effort in defense, and our threefold co-operation in economics (in trade, development and monetary policies), we shall inevitably strengthen our political ties as well. Just as your current efforts for unity in Europe will produce a stronger voice in the dialog between us, so in America our current battle for the liberty and prosperity of all our citizens can only deepen the meaning of our common historic purposes. In the far future, there may be a great new union for us all'.[5]

Breaking the silence: the European debate from the 1970s to the 1980s

The first cracks in this 'Atlantic silence' began to appear in the early 1970s, as three decades of more or less continuous economic growth came to an end. In the Federal Republic of Germany, Willy Brandt's policy of *Ostpolitik*, the attempt to create a less confrontational relationship between West and East Germany and, by implication, between western and eastern Europe, revived the possibility, however remote, of a Europe where the east-west ideological division might be less brutally enforced.[6] At the same time, the complex negotiations leading to the first EEC enlargement in 1973, which saw the UK, Denmark and the Republic of Ireland join the original six members, re-invigorated the old debate about Britain's place in Europe. The 1975 referendum on the UK's continued membership of the EEC, the result of an election pledge by the incoming Labour government, was contested as bitterly as any general election even though the rival 'yes' and 'no' campaigns cut across traditional party allegiances. The 'yes' campaign was supported by much of the political 'centre

---

[5] The reference to 'our current battle for the liberty and prosperity of all our citizens' was an allusion to the Civil Rights movement in the USA. The Paulskirche speech went far beyond the Declaration of Interdependence between Europe and the USA which Kennedy had announced the previous July in a speech at Independence Hall in Philadelphia. Both speeches are reproduced in full on the excellent American Presidency Project website at the University of California-Santa Barbara. See http://www.presidency.ucsb.edu/

[6] Timothy Garton Ash, *In Europe's Name: Germany and the Divided Continent* (London: Jonathan Cape, 1993).

ground', including the newly-elected leader of the Conservative Party, Margaret Thatcher. The 'no' campaign was endorsed by an ill-starred (non)alliance that included representatives from the left of the Labour Party, the right of the Conservative Party, the Ulster Unionists and assorted nationalists from Scotland and Wales. In the event, a large majority (67%) voted in favour of continued membership, though the fractured nature of the campaign probably tells us more about the labyrinthine complexities of British politics at the time than about any external European reality.[7]

As the global economic recession deepened, these localised debates gave way to a more sustained and general re-examination of the European project during the early and mid 1980s, a trend that has intensified ever since. The revival of the European debate was partly and paradoxically linked to the collapse of the post-war liberal consensus in Europe and the USA, itself a product of the economic recession. The election of 'new right' Conservative governments in the USA under Ronald Reagan and in the UK under Margaret Thatcher established a far more aggressive Atlantic alliance that brought the hesitant process of détente between the USA and the USSR to a shuddering halt, inaugurating what has been called the 'second Cold War'.[8] The neo-liberal economic and political agenda favoured in Washington and London was at odds with the consensual, social democratic orthodoxy still prevalent in western Europe, where a Socialist-Christian Democratic alliance led by French President François Mitterand and German Chancellor Helmut Kohl was now the backbone of a revived European federalism.

---

[7] Mark Baimbridge et al., *The 1975 Referendum on Europe* (2 Vols, Exeter: Imprint Academic Press, 2006). On the strange geography of this result, which saw the highest 'no' votes in Scotland and Northern Ireland, see Andrew M. Kirby and Peter J. Taylor, 'A geographical analysis of the voting pattern in the EEC referendum, 5 June 1975', *Regional Studies* 10, 2 (1976) pp. 183-191. It is worth noting here that the timing of the UK's entry into the EEC partially explains why such a large element in British political culture is still not reconciled with EU membership, despite their resounding defeat in 1975. The first decade of UK involvement coincided with the longest economic slump since the war, leading some Eurosceptics to conclude that membership of the European Community had worsened, or even caused, the UK's economic woes. The same constituency has since argued, rather more consistently, that the UK's economic recovery from the mid-1980s, which has undoubtedly been somewhat stronger than in many parts of the original EEC, has resulted from the distinctly 'un-European' neo-liberal solutions introduced during the 1980s to deal with the country's economic difficulties. From this perspective, the EU and its precursor institutions have been the principal cause of the UK's problems in the past and they bear no responsibility for any of its recent successes. This is the opposite of the argument generally accepted in most other European countries. For an interesting recent commentary, which makes some telling geographical points, see Timothy Garton Ash, 'Why Britain is in Europe', *Twentieth Century British History* 17 (2006) pp. 451-463.

[8] John Lewis Gaddis, *The Cold War* (London: Allen Lane, 2005). For an analysis informed by 'critical geopolitics', see Simon Dalby, *Creating the Second Cold War: The Discourse of Politics* (London: Routledge, 1990).

The chasm between the Anglo-American alliance and the Franco-German perspective, at once geopolitical and economic, revived the previously moribund European debate. Once the political implications of full economic union became clear, the long-running dispute between inter-governmental and federal perspectives on the European project, previously articulated in rather dry, technical terms and limited to the European institutions, was suddenly transformed into a visceral confrontation expressed in the language of personal and national identities. At the heart of this dispute was a fundamental difference of opinion about the meanings of sovereignty and citizenship. For inter-governmentalists, these were all-or-nothing, binary attributes. For federalists, they were malleable, 'poolable' concepts.

The inter-governmental perspective was famously championed by Margaret Thatcher who summarised her feelings with admirable clarity in a speech delivered in Bruges in September 1988. Here was the classic neo-liberal view of an open, flexible Europe of sovereign nation-states whose inter-relations should be determined by, and limited to, economic considerations and the desire for unfettered free trade between de-regulated, small state economies. Europe should be 'shallow' in governmental terms but as extensive geographically as was compatible with the security concerns of the USA and NATO. 'We (the UK government) have not successfully rolled back the frontiers of the state in Britain', Thatcher concluded, 'only to see them re-imposed at European level'.[9]

Thatcher's principal target was, of course, Jacques Delors, the President of the European Commission, and the physical embodiment of everything the UK Prime Minister despised about the European community. A French socialist, Delors was the architect of the 1987 Single European Act and the plan for full economic and monetary union, an unelected bureaucrat whose federalist agenda was explicitly based on the familiar idea of Europe supplanting the traditional nation-states. The Delors vision of Europe was expressed at greater length but with no less conviction in a speech delivered just over a year after Margaret Thatcher's address in exactly the same location in Bruges.[10]

The dispute between inter-governmentalism and federalism, though increasingly acrimonious, was not based on any fundamental difference of opinion about the potential geographical extent of Europe. Both sides had no choice but to recognise the geopolitical realities of a divided Europe though everyone paid lip-service to the

---

[9] The full text of the Bruges speech can readily be accessed on the website of the Bruges group, the predominantly right-wing Eurosceptic lobby group which now campaigns more or less openly for UK withdrawal from the EU. See http://www.brugesgroup.com

[10] The Delors speech is far more difficult to locate on the web and seems never to have been fully translated into English. Jacques Delors and Club Clisthène, *La France par l'Europe* (Paris: Grasset, 1998) reveals how the Delors vision is entirely consistent with the traditional view of Europe as the culmination of the French national project.

need for more economic and political connections between the two halves of the continent. Matters became more complicated however following the re-opening of dialogue about the future of Europe across the Cold War ideological division of the continent, a conversation facilitated by the growing tolerance of political debate in the Soviet Union and its satellite states. Dissident intellectuals in Czechoslovakia, Hungary and Poland were especially keen to re-assert their Europeanness and increasingly made use of a revived version of *Mitteleuropa* to justify their status as central, rather than eastern, Europeans. The 'return to Europe' debate, as it was sometimes called, was inspired in part by Solidarity's challenge to hard-line Communist rule in Poland but also drew on the memory of a richly cosmopolitan central European region that had been effaced by the 'scar of Yalta' when the region, and the whole of Europe, had been divided in 1945. This 'culture region' had not been destroyed it was claimed; merely silenced by the Cold War. The regional identity was already re-emerging, however, reinvigorated by a self-consciously post-modern language of cultural hybridity and multiple identities. Unlike earlier, more disturbing versions of *Mitteleuropa* developed in late 19th and early 20th century Germany, the 1980s version of this idea, formed outside of the German-speaking regions, emphasised the region's linguistic and cultural diversity as the 'heartland' of Europe where the cosmopolitan characteristics of the entire continent reached their highest level. Perhaps the outstanding commentary on this 1980s revival came from the Czech writer Milan Kundera in a justly famous 1984 essay on the 'tragedy of Central Europe'.[11]

The second new aspect of the European debate during the 1980s emanated from the Soviet Union itself, where Mikhail Gorbachev's cultural and political reforms included an explicit and sustained attempt to re-position the Russian heartland of the USSR as a self-consciously European zone, an idea that directly contradicted

---

[11] Milan Kundera, 'The tragedy of Central Europe', *New York Review of Books* 26th April 1984, pp. 439-461; and Hugh Seton-Watson, 'What is Europe? Where is Europe? From mystique to politique', *Encounter* 60, 2 (1985) pp. 9-17. Not everyone agreed that the idea of *Mitteleuropa* could escape its past. For critical commentaries on the 'return to Europe' debate, see Timothy Garton Ash, 'Mitteleuropa', *Daedalus* 119, 1 (1990) pp. 1-22; Tony Judt, *A Grand Illusion: An Essay on Europe* (London: Penguin, 1996) pp. 45-82; and Perry Anderson, 'The Europe to come', *London Review of Books* 25 January 1996. For recent analyses, see Hans-Georg Betz, 'Mitteleuropa and postmodern European identity', *New German Critique* 50 (1990) pp. 173-192; Jörg Brechtefeld, *Mitteleuropa and German Politics, 1848 to the Present* (London: Macmillan, 1996); Oskar Krejčí, *Geopolitics of the Central European Region: The View from Prague and Bratislava* (Bratislava: Veda, 2005); and Peter M. R. Stirk (ed.) *Mitteleuropa: History and Prospects* (Edinburgh: Edinburgh University Press, 1994). For recent geographical comments on the dilemmas of Central European identities, see Joshua Hagen, 'Redrawing the imagined map of Europe: the rise and fall of the "centre"', *Political Geography* 22 (2003) pp. 489-517; Merje Kuus, 'Ubiquitous identities and elusive subjects: puzzles from Central Europe', *Transactions of the Institute of British Geographers* 32, 1 (2007) pp. 90-101; and Merje Kuus, 'Intellectuals and geopolitics: the "cultural politicians" of Central Europe', *Geoforum* 37, 2 (2007) pp. 241-251.

previous Soviet policy. Extending the *Mitteleuropa* argument developed under the rallying cry of 'A Common European Home', the new Soviet leadership repeatedly insisted, in terms that echoed down the centuries to Catherine and Peter the Great, that Russia was historically, culturally, geopolitically (and even religiously) European in a way that the USA, forged in the struggle to free itself from European colonial authority, could never rightfully claim.[12]

New wine in old bottles: the European debate and European enlargement

By the end of the 1980s, the European debate was poised to develop in several new directions but few could have predicted the seismic changes that would follow. The unexpected collapse of the Soviet Union, the re-unification of Germany, and the break-up of other communist federations in east-central Europe transformed, in a few short months, the political map of Europe as well as the post-war geopolitical assumptions on which that map had been created. In the memorable words of François Mitterand in January 1990, 'Europe is returning to its history and its geography like one who is returning home'.[13] Suddenly, the hesitant stirrings of a new pan-European consciousness that might ultimately challenge the narrowly strategic Cold War idea of an Atlantic (western) Europe were replaced by wild speculations in a climate of euphoric optimism, particularly in Germany.

Initially, it seemed that western and eastern Europeans might be able to determine their own fate with minimal interference from the USA, now the only remaining superpower. George Bush Snr., America's first post-Cold War President, had promised at the beginning of his term in 1989 that he would 'not be a foreign policy President' overly dominated by traditional European concerns. The 'new world order' that came into being strengthened his understandable desire to cash the 'peace dividend' by scaling back the US military presence in western Europe.[14]

---

[12] Ivan Neumann, *Russia and the Idea of Europe: A Study in Identity and International Relations* (London: Routledge, 1996) pp. 131-193; and Ivan Neumann, *Uses of the Other: 'The East' in European Identity Formation* (Minneapolis: University of Minnesota Press, 1999). See also Paul Chilton and Mikhail Ilyin, 'Metaphor in political discourse: the case of the "Common European House"', *Discourse and Society* 4 (1993) pp. 7-31; Neil Malcolm, 'The "Common European House" and Soviet policy', *International Affairs* 65, 4 (1989) pp. 659-676.

[13] Quoted in Jacques Derrida, *The Other Heading: Reflections on Today's Europe* (Bloomington: Indianapolis University Press, 1992) p. 5.

[14] Martin Walker, 'Variable geography: America's mental maps of a greater Europe', *International Affairs* 76, 3 (2000) pp. 459-474. As Walker points out in this excellent analysis, Bill Clinton's first Secretary of State, Warren Christopher, reiterated the same view that American foreign policy had been 'too Eurocentric for too long'. It is worth noting here that the USA Congress elected in 1994 seemed unlikely to question the new sense of proportion in US relations with Europe. Over 100 members of the House of Representations did not possess a passport, and of those who did more had visited China than Europe. One consequence of the new American stance was a huge

The outbreak of war in the former Yugoslavia halted any putative moves towards US disengagement, though the US and EU attempts to bring an end to this first post-Cold War European conflict revealed the inadequacies in the traditional Atlantic alliance.[15] By the end of the 1990s, the USA had probably re-asserted whatever influence it had initially surrendered in Europe and was able to prevent moves towards an independent European defence and foreign policy to preserve the Atlantic alliance and ensure an enlarged NATO.[16] The continuing influence of the USA partially explains why the process of EU and NATO expansion into central and eastern Europe moved forward so rapidly over the next decade, despite the reservations of many senior western European politicians who would have preferred a slower and more cautious approach. These reservations, associated with an old-style federalist argument that the old EU should deepen rather than widen its economic and political integration, have been swept aside by a resurgent, globalising neo-liberal agenda adopted by most existing and aspiring EU countries.

In March 1998, the EU welcomed eleven states into the accession process, six of whom were deemed ready for fast-track membership on economic and socio-political grounds – Poland, Hungary, the Czech Republic, Slovenia, Estonia and Cyprus, the last based on a proviso regarding the division of the island. Five more countries were placed on a slower track – Lithuania, Latvia, Romania, Bulgaria and Slovakia, the last relegated largely out of concern about its authoritarian government. In the event, ten states were admitted in 2004 and two more – Bulgaria and Romania – joined in 2007. It remains to be seen how these changes will impact on the economic geography of an enlarged EU.[17]

---

reduction in the State Department's budget to cover foreign aid, diplomacy, the UN and all other international organizations. This slumped to an all-time low of barely one per cent of the federal budget in the mid-1990s. Walker's 'mental maps' can be usefully compared with an earlier 'geographical' analysis of American foreign policy priorities before the end of the Cold War in Alan K. Hendrikson, 'The geographical "mental maps" of American foreign policymakers', *International Political Science Review* 1, 4 (1980) pp. 495-530.

[15] David Campbell, *National Deconstruction: Violence, Identity and Justice in Bosnia* (Minneapolis: University of Minnesota Press, 1997); Laura Silber and Allan Little, *The Death of Yugoslavia* (London: Penguin, 1995).

[16] See Peter van Ham, 'Europe's common defence policy: implications for the trans-Atlantic relationship', *Security Dialogue* 31 (2000) pp. 215-228.

[17] Many economic geographers argue that enlargement is likely to exacerbate regional economic and political divisions if the EU enforces a more neo-liberal economic agenda. The presence of a 'core' Euro-zone, comprising nearly half of all EU states and well over half the total population, also threatens to intensify rather than diminish regional divisions. See John Agnew, 'How many Europes? The European Union, eastward enlargement and uneven development', *European Urban and Regional Studies* 8, 1 (2001) pp. 29-38; Mick Dunford, 'Old Europe, New Europe and the USA: comparative economic performance, inequality and the market-led model of development', *European Urban and Regional Studies* 12 (2005) pp. 149-176; Ron Martin, 'EMU versus the regions? Regional convergence and divergence in Euroland', *Journal of Economic Geography* 1 (2001) pp. 51-80.

Freed from the constraints imposed by the Cold War, it is striking how quickly the discussions about EU enlargement fell back on the foundational narratives discussed in chapter one, with both positive and negative implications. The traditional politico-legal definition of Europe – the idea that Europe is a space where enlightened values are enshrined in law – has clearly influenced the pace, nature and direction of enlargement as decisions have hinged on the willingness of aspiring member states to demonstrate a verifiable commitment to democratic government, civil liberties and respect for human rights. For Euro-enthusiasts, this is an entirely positive process for it demonstrates the EU's unique capacity to spread desirable political practices in countries where there was little or no tradition of democratic government until the 1990s. Unlike traditional empires that have sought to spread their 'civilised' values by force, often with disastrous consequences, the EU has expanded by invitation and has enforced democracy and human rights by legal example, persuasion and a kind of benign, disciplinary moral presence.[18]

Unfortunately, this same process can also degenerate into a less edifying 21st century version of the exclusive Christian and civilisational geopolitics described in chapter one. This is especially evident in the EU's relations with Russia and Turkey and in its policies on immigration. In the Russian case, the rush to enlarge both the EU and NATO into the former Soviet realm has created predictable difficulties and an anti-Russian sentiment that has long defined European unity but which many had hoped would fade in the post-Communist era.[19] Unfortunately, the prospect of old-style economic warfare whereby Russian withholds its energy resources and Europe closes its markets cannot be entirely ruled out.[20]

In the Turkish case, the most ancient element in the European mythology, anti-Muslim prejudice, has re-surfaced with a vengeance. As I mentioned in chapter one, a number of prominent European politicians in France and Germany, including the former French President and author of the EU Constitution Valéry Giscard d'Estaing, have adopted a particularly hard line against Turkey's potential membership of the EU, even though this was accepted in principle at the Helsinki

---

[18] This argument is persuasively developed by Mark Leonard, *Why Europe will Run the 21st Century* (London: Fourth Estate, 2005) pp. 35-48. The Council of Europe has reinforced the same disciplines on an even larger group of countries, including Turkey and Russia. The USA would not, of course, qualify for membership of the Council of Europe, even if eligible on geographical grounds, as it retains the death penalty in many states. Of the 41 member states of the Council, however, 39 have rejected the death penalty and two (Russia and Turkey) have imposed a moratorium on its use.

[19] The political and cultural implications of NATO expansion are imaginatively explored in Merje Kuus, 'Love, peace and Nato? Imperial subject-making in Central Europe, *Antipode* 39, 2 (2007) pp. 269-290. See also Merje Kuus, 'Europe's eastern enlargement and the re-inscription of otherness in East-Central Europe', *Progress in Human Geography* 18, 4 (2004) pp. 472-489.

[20] Debra Johnson and Paul Robinson (eds.) *Perspectives on EU-Russia Relations* (London: Routledge, 2005).

Summit in 1999. The negotiations have proceeded with glacial slowness ever since due to opposition from the anti-Turkish European lobby, currently led by the newly-elected French President Nicolas Sarkozy, and from Eurosceptics in Turkey itself.[21] The European opponents of Turkey's membership of the EU make few attempts to disguise their belief that this would compromise their definition of Europe as a predominantly Christian space where Muslims can be tolerated only as immigrants or as permanent citizens of existing states.[22]

In the case of EU immigration controls, the contrast between the liberal attitude towards migration within the community and the increasingly complex and selective procedures now being imposed on immigrants from beyond its borders suggests that the EU is unable to develop policies that do not simply replicate the 'closed space' thinking of its constituent nation-states.[23] Put simply, the process of EU enlargement has revealed the persistence of the fundamental dilemma of the European debate discussed in chapter one – the contradictory desire to define Europe according to the loftiest, supposedly universal principles while also using these same principles to exclude races, religions and nations who are deemed inherently un-European.

The coming polity? The Habermas-Derrida declaration

One might be tempted to conclude from this that for all its apparent complexity and sophistication the European debate has made perilously little advance in recent years. Today's politicians are still prone to re-cycle the most ancient essentialising myths about the region whenever they claim to act in Europe's name. This is unlikely to

---

[21] Chris Rumford, 'From Luxembourg to Helsinki: Turkey, the politics of EU enlargement and the prospects of accession', *Contemporary Politics* 6, 4 (2000) pp. 331-343. It is worth emphasising that the US campaigned to keep open the possibility of Turkey's membership of the EU in the 1990s, despite French and Germany hostility, in order to ensure the country's continuing allegiance within NATO.

[22] Ziya Öniş, 'Domestic politics, international norms and challenges to the state: Turkey-EU relations in the post-Helsinki era', *Turkish Studies* 4, 1 (2003) pp. 9-34.

[23] The European Commission's *Green Paper on an EU Approach to Managing Economic Migration* (Brussels: CEC, 2005) is a revealing example of the difficulties facing the EU in this respect. For recent commentaries, see Adrian Favell and Randall Hansen, 'Markets against politics: migration, EU enlargement and the idea of Europe', *Journal of Ethnic and Migration Studies* 28, 4 (2002) pp. 581-601; Henk von Houtum and Roos Pijpers, 'The European Union as a gated community: the two-faced border immigration control of the EU', *Antipode* 39, 2 (2007) pp. 291-309; and Michael Samers, 'An emerging geopolitics of "illegal" immigration in the EU', *European Journal of Migration and Law* 6, 1 (2004) pp. 27-45. See also the related work on border regions themselves by Lila Leontidou, Hastings Donnan and Alex Afouxenidis, 'Exclusion and difference along the EU border: social and cultural markers, spatialities and mappings', *International Journal of Urban and Regional Research* 29, 2 (2005) pp. 389-407; Lila Leontidou, 'The boundaries of Europe: deconstructing three regional narratives', *Identities: Global Studies in Culture and Power* 11 (2004) pp. 593-617.

change in the immediate future, of course, for it is in the nature of politicians to rely on crude over-simplifications. But those eager to see a different and more progressive vision of Europe for the 21st century world may derive at least some comfort from the potentially significant developments in the European debate in the past decade or so. These discussions would probably have excited minimal interest were it not for the events of September 11th 2001 and the subsequent transformation of American foreign policy, particularly in respect of the Muslim world. If the end of the Cold War and the re-unification of Europe revived a moribund European debate, the fall-out from 9/11 may end up shifting the terms of this debate in a radically new direction. Prior to the September attacks, the USA had remained a key influence shaping the European debate *from within*. The USA was a European presence and a European military power. Since 9/11, the assumption that the USA ultimately represents European interests as well as it own has been subjected to more serious and sustained questioning than at any time since 1945. For many Europeans, this assumption simply cannot be justified given the unilateral inclinations and actions of the current US administration. There is a palpable sense that Europe and the USA now reflect two quite separate and diverging political cultures.

This has not yet generated a complete rupture, of course, but the 'war on terror' launched by President George Bush Jnr. and the subsequent US and UK-led invasions of Afghanistan and Iraq have opened up serious splits within the European Union (both actual and potential) between the latent pro- and anti-American perspectives (between the 'new' and 'old' Europes in the language of US Secretary of Defense Donald Rumsfeld). The desperate attempts by the previous UK government under Tony Blair to stitch together an alliance within Europe and the United Nations that might hold together the Atlantic alliance seems to have failed, mainly because the Bush administration has displayed a quite extraordinary indifference to maintaining this long-cherished fulcrum of American foreign policy. This is indeed a remarkable transformation which threatens to remove, for the first time since World War Two, the Atlantic context within which all European debates have previously been conducted.

Turning point though 9/11 undoubtedly was, it is important to recognise that many of the 'neo-conservative' advisers who surround the current US President George Bush Jnr had already expressed deep scepticism that the Atlantic alliance could survive as an equal partnership between the USA and a fully integrated and enlarged Europe. From this perspective, an enlarged united Europe was never likely to be compatible with America's global economic and strategic interests. The Harvard-based conservative political scientist Samuel Huntington warned in 1992 that 'The political integration of the European Community, if that should occur, would bring into existence an extraordinarily powerful entity which could not help but be perceived as a major threat to American interests'. The USA should therefore promote what Huntington called the 'evolution of the European Community in the direction of a looser, purely economic entity with broader membership rather than a tighter political entity with an integrated foreign… and possibly defense policy'.[24]

At the other end of the 1990s, another 'neo-con' theorist, John Bolton, then Senior Vice President of the American Enterprise Institute, insisted before the US House of Representatives Committee on International Relations in November 1999 that 'the aim to align the foreign and defense policies of the EU's members into one shared and uniform policy is at times motivated by a desire to distance themselves from US influence, or in some cases by openly anti-American intentions'.[25] Faced with this kind of provocation, the USA should not hesitate to develop its own anti-EU policies.

In between these two statements, conservative American political journals such as *The National Interest* were openly encouraging British withdrawal from all but the free trading system of the EU and the establishment of a new union of English-speaking peoples.[26] The advent of the euro served only to intensify right-wing American hostility to all aspects of the European project in the late 1990s. According to the exceptionally bleak predictions of the Harvard economist Martin Feldstein, the introduction of the euro was an unmitigated disaster for the USA and risked unleashing warfare and destruction in Europe itself.[27]

---

[24] Quoted in John L. Harper, *American Visions of Europe: Franklin D. Roosevelt, George F. Kennan and Dean G. Acheson* (Cambridge: Cambridge University Press, 1996) p. 335. Huntington is, of course, a key influence on neo-conservative American thinking. See his best-selling book *The Clash of Civilizations and the Remaking of World Order* (London: Simon and Schuster, 1997) which predicted a return to a quasi-Medieval civilisational geopolitics characterised by conflict between religious and cultural groupings rather than nation-states. The phrase 'the clash of civilisations', which Huntington first used as the title for an article in *Foreign Affairs* published in 1993, was coined by another academic guru of the American far right, the historian Bernard Lewis, in a 1990 article in *The Atlantic Monthly* on 'The roots of Muslim rage', likewise expanded into a book with the same title.

[25] Quoted in Walker, 'Variable geography' *op. cit.*, p. 471. This is, of course, the same John Bolton who served briefly and controversially as US Ambassador to the United Nations from August 2005 to December 2006.

[26] The renewed interest in an 'English-speaking union' or 'Anglosphere', an idea based explicitly on arguments developed by members of the Round Table in the early 20th century, has been proposed by several Anglo-American intellectuals, notably the conservative historian of the Soviet Union Robert Conquest. See his 'Toward an English speaking union', *The National Interest* 57 (1999) pp. 64-70.

[27] Martin Feldstein, 'EMU and international conflict', *Foreign Affairs* 76, 6 (1997) pp. 60-73. Given the apocalyptic nature of these predictions, which have mercifully failed to materialise thus far, it is perhaps a cause for concern that Feldstein, who was Ronald Reagan's chief economic adviser, has recently been appointed to the US Foreign Intelligence Advisory Board. For a more measured assessment of the growing sense of US-EU divergence in the late 1990s, see the comments by Feldstein's Harvard colleague Joseph S. Nye, 'The US and Europe: continental drift', *International Affairs* 76, 1 (2000) pp. 51-60.

Since 9/11, a number of intriguing new proposals have been advanced within Europe itself, calling explicitly for a more assertive and independent European foreign policy to counterbalance the American perspective. Indeed, the debate has widened to include calls for a new European constitution that would express as clearly as possible what is distinctive about a 21st century European political culture, unshackled from the continent's own recent past and from the policies and interests of the USA. An otherwise unlikely pairing of Jürgen Habermas, the last representative of the Frankfurt School, arch defender of the ideals of the European Enlightenment, and leading theoretician of communication and consensus, and Jacques Derrida, the playful poststructuralist, opponent of consensus, and doyen of deconstruction, generated one of the more remarkable contributions to this debate.

On 31st May 2003, a few months after the first draft of the EU Constitution was unveiled by Valéry Giscard d'Estaing, Habermas and Derrida issued a joint declaration, published in German in the *Frankfurter Allgemeine Zeitung* and in French in *Libération*, entitled 'After the War: The Rebirth of Europe'. This text, which was written by Habermas and merely endorsed by Derrida, was a direct response to the letter signed by some European leaders, including Tony Blair, Silvio Berlusconi, José María Aznar and Václav Havel on 31st January 2003 endorsing the build-up of American pressure on Iraq. Building on a selection of dialogues conducted in the immediate aftermath of 9/11 between Habermas, Derrida and the US-based Italian philosopher Giovanna Borradori, the declaration argued for a unified European foreign policy 'to balance out the hegemonic unilateralism of the United States' and co-ordinated European activity within the UN.[28]

The independent EU foreign policy envisaged by Habermas and Derrida was framed in the context of a re-articulated European identity. The timing was right, it was argued, because the spontaneous outpouring of public indignation on 15th February 2003 – 'the day on which the demonstrating masses in London and Rome, Madrid and Barcelona, Berlin and Paris' had reacted collectively to the preparations for an American-led onslaught against Iraq – had already indicated the existence of an assertive European consciousness. Drawing explicitly on Kant's concept of *Weltinnenpolitik*, the idea of cosmopolitan, shared world politics ensured by international law, the Habermas-Derrida manifesto argued that 15th February marked

---

[28] Jürgen Habermas and Jacques Derrida, 'February 15, or what binds Europeans together: a plea for a common foreign policy, beginning in core Europe', *Constellations* 10 (2003) pp. 291-297. The conversations with Borradori have since been published as Giovanni Borradori, *Philosophy in a Time of Terror: Dialogues with Jürgen Habermas and Jacques Derrida* (Chicago: University of Chicago Press, 2003). The original Habermas-Derrida declaration is re-printed in Daniel Levy, Max Pensky and John Torpey (eds.) *Old Europe, New Europe, Core Europe: Transatlantic Relations after the Iraq War* (London: Verso, 2005) pp. 3-13.

'the birth of a *Europäische Öffentlichkeit*', the origins of a new European public sphere.[29]

Europe should not meekly accept its inferior position as defined by the 20th century Atlantic alliance, the declaration continued. Rather, the European peoples should embrace a new constitution recognising and celebrating four distinctively European political and cultural achievements, the building blocks of new, pan-European identity. These are: a) the neutrality of authority (embodied in the separation of church and state); b) the faith in the power of politics and a relatively benign state to ameliorate the impact of unfettered capitalism; c) the ethos of solidarity that emerges from a collective struggle to ensure a greater measure of social justice; d) the high esteem accorded to international law and the rights of the individual.

According to Habermas and Derrida, these four characteristics are already well established in the 'core' European states and are in the process of being fully embedded in the 'new' European countries of the former Soviet empire. These are not abstract ideals, insist Habermas and Derrida, but universally endorsed, concrete values and expectations in most parts of Europe. They are the building blocks of what Habermas has previously called 'constitutional patriotism'.[30] They bind European societies together, even while other forces keep them apart. These characteristics have allowed western Europe simultaneously to solve political and social problems that have proved too difficult for successive US administrations operating in a different political culture. It is Europe, rather than the USA that has established a genuinely supranational political order through the EU, while preserving a powerful form of a social justice through the welfare state. It is Europe, rather than the USA, that has developed a workable 'post-national political culture' that allows 'governance beyond the traditional nation state' and that serves as an exemplar for other regions. And it is Europe, rather than the USA, that has become a genuinely transformative influence in spreading democratic ideals and human rights through the disciplines and legal obligations the EU imposes on its members, aspiring members and trading partners. The European Union acts in a radically different way from the USA, assert Habermas and Derrida, because it has few of the characteristics of a traditional nation-state or empire whereas the USA retains most if not all of

---

[29] For a discussion of Kant's original formulation, see Martha Nussbaum, 'Kant and stoic cosmopolitanism', *Journal of Political Philosophy* 5, 1 (1997) pp. 1-25; and James Tully, 'The Kantian idea of Europe: critical and cosmopolitan perspectives', in Anthony Pagden (ed.) *The Idea of Europe: From Antiquity to the European Union* (Cambridge: Cambridge University Press, 2002) pp. 331-358.

[30] Jürgen Habermas, 'Struggles for recognition in the democratic constitutional state', in *The Inclusion of the Other: Studies in Political Theory* (Cambridge, MA: MIT Press, 1998) pp. 225-226. For a commentary, see Craig Calhoun, 'Constitutional patriotism and the public sphere: interests, identity, and solidarity in the integration of Europe', in Pablo de Greiff and Ciaran Cronin (eds.) *Global Justice and Transnational Politics* (Cambridge, MA: MIT Press, 2002) pp. 275-312.

these characteristics. A new EU constitution would clarify and encourage Europe's distinctive role in the world.[31]

According to Habermas and Derrida, the differences between the EU and the USA stem from historical divergences between Europe and the USA since World War Two. The centralising power of the US government was strengthened during World War Two and never adequately redressed after 1945. In Europe, by contrast, the war and its aftermath underlined the need to pool resources of capital and labour for the collective good. Likewise, the experiences of colonial governance, and more especially decolonisation, have taught Europeans a more sensitive 'reflective distance' with respect to the non-European communities within their midst. This has fostered an emerging pan-European culture that is more genuinely cosmopolitan than that of the USA where ethnic identities have proved stubbornly resistant to more than a century of American assimilation. Europe cannot claim to have achieved this ideal state, to be sure, but the new Europe can and should continually aspire to develop a cosmopolitan political culture and already has a series of powerful traditions on which to draw. Indeed, it is this aspiration which ultimately defines what it means to be a European, and this should form the basis of a European constitution.

The Habermas-Derrida proclamation was a remarkable document, a conscious attempt to update the traditional, exclusionary idea of Europe for the 21st century by emphasising the distinctiveness of Europe's modern, multi-ethnic political culture (both actual and potential, being and becoming) from that of the USA. While the proclamation was written in direct response to the apparent break-down of the Atlantic alliance after 9/11 and the resulting shift in US foreign policy, it is important to emphasise that these ideas reflect on-going debates about the ethical and moral frameworks within which a new European identity might be forged. Just as the American reaction to 9/11 was foreshadowed by the pre-existing 'neo-con' intellectual revolution in the USA, so the Habermas-Derrida statement reflected a longer historical gestation of these sentiments in Europe.

For Habermas, the proclamation was an entirely logical extension of his well-known historical work on the transformative role of the public sphere which he has applied consistently to contemporary European politics.[32] The decision to compose and publish the declaration was clearly intended to stimulate debate about ideas that Habermas had been advancing for some time in the hope these might also influence the debate about the real EU Constitution. The involvement of the late Jacques

---

[31] See, for an earlier argument, Jürgen Habermas, 'Why Europe needs a constitution', *New Left Review* 11 (2001) pp. 5-26.

[32] Jürgen Habermas, *The Structural Transformation of the Public Sphere: An Inquiry into a Category of Bourgeois Society* (Cambridge, MA: MIT Press, 1991, originally published in 1962). For an unflinching but sympathetic commentary, see Craig Calhoun, *Habermas and the Public Sphere* (Cambridge, MA: Harvard University Press, 1992).

Derrida was in many respects more intriguing because the idea of deconstruction with which he is so closely associated is often seen as an exemplification of the post-structural assault on the Enlightenment project and, by implication, on the very idea of Europe as a culturally and politically distinctive region. And yet Derrida spent the last 15 years of his life working on what he called 'the heritage' or 'inheritance' (depending on translation) of post-Enlightenment thinking in order to clarify some key concepts on which a new philosophy of ethics and a new 'politics of acknowledgment' might be established. Some of the themes Derrida explored involved large moral questions associated with the law, justice, and the death penalty but he also wrote on more intimate but no less profound subjects such as friendship, gifts and gift-giving, testimony, confession, mourning, forgiveness, and – of most direct relevance to his interest in a future European politics – hospitality.[33] Derrida's work on the idea of hospitality and asylum, ideas rooted in traditional Christian and Islamic religious practices, emerged from his earlier thought experiments on the possibility of creating 'cities of refuge', as alternatives to the traditional, territorial nation-states where some of the key problems of immigration and social and ethnic difference might be resolved in new and more imaginative ways.[34]

So, lest there be any doubt about the matter, both Habermas and Derrida were developing comparable and interwoven projects about the possibility of a new European political culture from the early 1990s. Thus we find Habermas insisting in 1992 on the need to build a new European identity freed from the constraints of the past but fully cognisant of its lessons: 'our task is less to reassure ourselves of our common origins in the European Middle Ages', he wrote, 'than to develop a new political self-confidence commensurate with the role of Europe in the world of the twenty-first century. Hitherto, world history has accorded the empires that have come and gone only *one* appearance on the stage… It now appears as if Europe as a whole is being given a second chance. It will not be able to make use of this in terms of the power politics of yesteryear, but only under changed premises, namely a non-imperial process of reaching understanding with, and learning from, other cultures'.[35]

---

[33] See, for example, Jacques Derrida, *De l'hospitalité* (Paris: Calmann-Lévy, 1997); Jacques Derrida, *Cosmopolites de tous les pays, encore un effort!* (Paris: Galilée, 1997); and Jacques Derrida, *Foi et savoir, suivi de Le siècle et le pardon: entretien avec Michel Wieviorka* (Paris: Éditions du Seuil, 2000). For translations, see Jacques Derrida, *Of Hospitality* (Stanford: Stanford University Press, 2000) and Jacques Derrida, *On Cosmopolitanism and Forgiveness* (London: Routledge, 2001).

[34] For a related discussion, see Michael Shapiro, 'The events of discourse and the ethics of global hospitality', *Millennium: Journal of International Studies* 27, 3 (1998) pp. 695-713. Julia Kristeva makes the telling point that the word hospitality has its roots in the Greek definition of 'ethos' as the habit of providing and accepting regular shelter. See Julia Kristeva, 'Europhilia, Europhobia', *Constellations* 5, 3 (1998) pp. 321-332.

[35] Jürgen Habermas, 'Citizenship and national identity: some reflections on the future of Europe', *Praxis International* 12, 1 (1992) pp. 1-19.

In the same year, Derrida was insisting that 'It is necessary to make ourselves the guardians of an idea of Europe, of a different Europe, a Europe that consists precisely in not closing itself off in its own identity'.[36]

In his last interview before his death in October 2004, Derrida returned to the European theme. His remarks are worth quoting at length: 'I believe that it is without Eurocentric illusions or pretensions, without a trace of European nationalism, indeed without even an excess of confidence in Europe as it now is (or appears in the process of becoming), that we must fight for what this name represents today, with the memory of the Enlightenment, to be sure, but also with the full awareness – and the full admission – of the totalitarian, genocidal and colonialist crimes of the past. We must fight for what is irreplaceable within Europe in the world to come, so that it might become more than just a single market or single currency, more than a neo-nationalist conglomerate, more than a new military power. This would be a Europe where one can criticise Israeli politics… without being accused of anti-Semitism or Judeophobia; a Europe where one can support the legitimate aspirations of the Palestinian people to recover their rights, lands and state, without condoning suicide attacks;… a Europe where one can express concern about the rise of both anti-Semitism and Islamophobia;… a Europe where one can criticise the initiatives of Bush, Cheney, Wolfowitz and Rumsfeld without countenancing in the least the horrors of the Saddam Hussein regime; a Europe where, without anti-Americanism, without anti-Israelism, without anti-Palestinian Islamophobia, one can ally oneself with those who, whether American, Israeli, or Palestinian, courageously criticise… the governments or dominant forces of their own countries… That is my dream'.[37]

Cosmopolitanism now?

The Habermas-Derrida declaration provoked a lively debate, beginning with a series of articles published, at Habermas's instigation, in different European newspapers on the same day as the original statement. These included short essays by Umberto Eco in *La Repubblica*, Adolf Muschg in *Neue Zürcher Zeitung*, Gianni Vattimo in *La Stampa*, Fernando Savater in *El País*, and Richard Rorty in *Süddeutsche Zeitung*.[38] According to the last-named, the Habermas-Derrida declaration deserved support if only because it might ultimately reinforce liberal ideals in the USA which Rorty believed to be under serious threat in the wake of 9/11.[39]

---

[36] Jacques Derrida, *The Other Heading: Reflections on Today's Europe* (Bloomington: Indianapolis University Press, 1992) (originally published as *L'Autre Cap* (Paris: Éditions de Minuit, 1991) p. 29.

[37] Jacques Derrida, 'Une Europe de l'espoir', *Le Monde Diplomatique* 3 November 2004.

[38] These articles are translated in Levy *et al.*, Old Europe, New Europe *op. cit.*, pp. 14-43.

[39] Richard Rorty, 'Humiliation or solidarity', in Levy *et al.*, Old Europe, New Europe *op. cit.*, pp. 34-40.

But it is the cosmopolitanism at the core of the Habermas-Derrida declaration that has attracted the most critical attention, drawing on a range of earlier writings as well. It has been argued that a new European cosmopolitanism, like the new Europe itself, would need to develop simultaneously with and beyond the traditional meaning of this term, as derived from Kant and other Enlightenment and pre-Enlightenment sources.[40] The objective would be a distinctively European 'cosmopolitics', enshrined in law and in a European constitution, that might energise the Habermasian concept of 'constitutional patriotism'.[41]

Supporters of the original proposal have attempted to specify some practical implications, notably Ulrich Beck and Anthony Giddens.[42] Their accounts differ in significant ways but start from the premise that Europe will inevitably have to respond to an increasingly globalised world and will therefore have to re-invent itself as a meaningful cultural and political concept. In doing so, the traditional idea of Europe should not be entirely abandoned, however, for some of its foundational narratives contain enabling concepts worth reviving and modernising. Even the darker chapters in Europe's history should be regarded as a usable resource, a way of shaping collective action in the future. Beck's analysis, informed by the *Historikerstreit* (the German attempt to come to terms with an 'unmasterable' Nazi past),[43] is especially significant in this respect for he openly advocates the idea of a 21st century Europe as a new cosmopolitan *empire*.[44] The word 'empire' has shockingly negative connotations, of course, but Beck insists that the word should be used despite and

---

[40] See Nussbaum, 'Kant and stoic cosmopolitanism' *op. cit.* and Tully, 'The Kantian idea of Europe', *op. cit.*

[41] For Derrida's own perspectives, see Derrida, On Cosmopolitanism and Forgiveness *op. cit.* See also Kwame Anthony Appiah, *Cosmopolitanism: Ethics in a World of Strangers* (New York: W. W. Norton, 2006); Ulrich Beck, *Cosmopolitan Vision* (Cambridge: Polity Press, 2006); Tim Brennan, *At Home in the World: Cosmopolitanism Now* (Cambridge, Mass.: Harvard University Press, 1997); Pheng Cheah and Bruce Robbins (eds.) *Cosmopolitics: Thinking and Feeling Beyond the Nation* (Minneapolis: University of Minesota Press, 1998); David Held, *Democracy and Global Order from the Modern State to Cosmopolitan Governance* (Stanford: Stanford University Press, 1995); Thomas W. Pogge, 'Cosmopolitanism and sovereignty', *Ethics* 103 (1992) pp. 48-75; and Stephen Toulmin, *Cosmopolis: The Hidden Agenda of Modernity* (Chicago: The University of Chicago Press, 1990). For a more sustained geographical treatment, see Yi-Fu Tuan, *Cosmos and Hearth: A Cosmopolite's Viewpoint* (Minneapolis: University of Minnesota Press, 1996).

[42] Ulrich Beck and Edgar Grande, *Cosmopolitan Europe* (Cambridge: Polity Press, 2007); Ulrick Beck and Edgar Grande, 'Cosmopolitanism: Europe's way out of the crisis', *European Journal of Social Theory* 10 (2007) pp. 67-85; and Anthony Giddens, *Europe in the Global Age* (Cambridge: Polity Press, 2007). See also the perceptive remarks, which relate directly to Europe, by J. Nicholas Entrikin, 'Political community, identity and cosmopolitan place', *International Sociology* 14, 3 (1999) pp. 269-282.

[43] The literature is vast but see Charles S. Maier, *The Unmasterable Past: History, Holocaust, and German National Identity* (Cambridge, MA: Harvard University Press, 1988).

[44] The French edition of Beck and Grande's *Cosmopolitan Europe* pulls no punches and is entitled simply *Pour un empire européen* (Paris: Flammarion, 2007).

because of this history, in full cognisance of its less progressive historical associations, to be sure, but also aware of the utopian cosmopolitanism that informed the early 20th century campaign to reform an Anglo-centric British Empire into a federal British Commonwealth, for example, or the comparable and contemporaneous debates about the possibility of reforming the Austro-Hungarian empire to protect and enhance its cosmopolitan character. In using this phrase, Beck is seeking to re-habilitate not only the idea of Europe but the idea of empire as well.[45]

These very recent writings on a potential European future are seeking nothing less than a solution to the same fundamental dilemma that has beset the Europe debate since its origins. The objective is to define Europe according to the most desirable and inspirational universal principles of human rights while ensuring that these same principles are not used to create an exclusive, enclosed Europe, sealed off from the 'others' who live beyond its borders. The starting point is not to decide in advance who qualifies as a European or where Europe's limits are located. Rather, it is to re-define what it means to be European in consciously non-exclusive terms. One could imagine a not too distant future, suggests Ash Amin, where 'empathy [and] engagement with the stranger could become the essence of what it is to be European'.[46]

The idea of Europe in the 21st century would thus be re-defined so as to remain open to the influence and impact of those other cultures which may not belong to the 'core' European traditions but are nevertheless present in European societies. This would be a Europe that would no longer need to be defined, as it has traditionally been, by reference to an external, threatening 'other'. This would be a genuinely cosmopolitan Europe, with greater power allocated to regional scale, sub-national government but with the European scale of governance determining and ensuring the constitutional rights and responsibilities of all European citizens. Rights of citizenship, including equal access to the law, welfare, education and health, would need to be uncoupled from nationality (as defined by the range of 'old' criteria that currently still exist in different European states such as birthplace, ethnicity and even language) and defined instead by a minimum period of residence.[47] According to

---

[45] This echoes recent revisionist histories of the British imperialism which have emphasised empire as a space of mutually beneficial innovation, experimentation and exchange that was often entirely positive for colonisers and colonised alike. There is more than a hint of this revisionism in David Cannadine, *Ornamentalism: How the British Saw Their Empire* (London: Allen Lane, 2001) though it reaches its zenith in Niall Ferguson, *Empire: How Britain Made the Modern World* (London: Allen Lane, 2004).

[46] Ash Amin, 'Multi-ethnicity and the idea of Europe', *Theory, Culture and Society* 21, 2 (2004) pp. 1-24, quotation on p. 3.

[47] Seyla Benhabib, 'Citizens, residents, and aliens in a changing world: political membership in the global era', *Social Research* 66, 3 (1999) pp. 709-744.

Amin, this would be 'a Europe of minorities and minor belongings, stripped free of an old baggage of Eurocentric values' but nevertheless made real and concrete by a solid 'bedrock of constitutional rights'.[48]

This does not mean an 'anything goes' relaxation of all immigration controls, for example, for Derrida's philosophical inquiries on hospitality and the gift-giving make it clear that there is a double or contradictory imperative at the heart of the cosmopolitan ideal. An unconditional hospitality that insists on the need to offer refuge to all immigrants and newcomers, regardless of circumstances is immediately undermined by the obvious fact that hospitality has to be conditional otherwise the categories involved in the transaction, the inescapable difference between the giver and the receiver of hospitality, collapse. In other words, there has to be some limitation on the rights of residence otherwise the very idea of hospitality – and by implication cosmopolitanism – become meaningless. Derrida offered no easy solution to this dilemma, relying on the somewhat vague suggestion that European legislators think continuously, in concrete and practical terms, about this problem and ensure that the law operates within the space between these logical oppositions: 'It is a question of knowing how to transform and improve the law, and of knowing if this improvement is possible within an historical space which takes place between the law of an unconditional hospitality, offered a priori to every other, to all newcomers, whoever they may be, and the conditional laws of a right to hospitality, without which the unconditional law of hospitality would be in danger of remaining a pious and irresponsible desire, without form and without potency, and of even being perverted at any moment'.[49]

The Habermas-Derrida declaration, and the associated literature on cosmopolitanism, has also generated a good deal of criticism, much of it warranted. Within a few months of its appearance, dozens of writers and academics had commented on the declaration, some supportive, many critical.[50] Scornful critics on the right (in Europe as well as the USA) attacked it as vague, wishful thinking that simply ignored the inconvenient resilience of anti-EU European 'patriotism' and the continuing need for an Atlantic alliance in a new and more unpredictable 21st century world.[51]

---

[48] Amin, 'Multi-ethnicity and the idea of Europe' *op. cit.*, p. 22.

[49] Derrida, On Cosmopolitanism and Forgiveness *op. cit.*, pp. 22-23. For excellent discussions from an explicitly geographical perspectives, see Clive Barnett, 'Ways of relating: hospitality and the acknowledgement of otherness', *Progress in Human Geography* 29 (2005) pp. 1-17; Mustafa Dikeç, 'Pera peras poros: longings for spaces of hospitality', *Theory, Culture and Society* 19, 1-2 (2002) pp. 227-247; Claude Raffestin, 'Réinventer l'hospitalité', *Communications* 65 (1997) pp. 165-177.

[50] Levy *et al.*, Old Europe, New Europe *op. cit.*, pp. 47-22 reproduce 26 contributions in all, ranging from Ulrich Beck to Susan Sontag, the majority of which were published in German newspapers.

[51] See, for example, Helen Szamuely, 'Intellectual mind games', on the Bruges Group website – http://www.brugesgroup.com

The claim that a new European identity could be defined in the absence of a constituting 'other' has also been vigorously challenged, particularly by American critics who reached the not altogether surprising conclusion that the Habermas-Derrida declaration was motivated by an anti-American desire to challenge the global power of the USA. Advocates of the new Europe have rejected charges of generic anti-Americanism, insisting their opposition is directed solely towards the current US administration, but despite these protestations of innocence, it is difficult to avoid the impression that the new Europe is being defined, like all earlier visions of a united Europe, by reference to a non-European 'other', in this case the USA.[52] One does not need to be a die-hard defender of the traditional Atlantic alliance to find this a deeply troubling idea.

Others have expressed concern that a new Europe characterised by what Craig Calhoun has called 'thin identities and normative universalism' would be defined solely by an abstract, austere constitutionalism that would merely invoke legal definitions of cosmopolitanism rather than create a new European consciousness on the ground.[53] Defenders of the new idea of Europe insist that one can already detect a form of 'banal cosmopolitanism' in most parts of the continent – what Tony Judt has called 'Europe as a way of life'.[54] This is associated with the everyday passions and pastimes of sport, fashion, food, music, film, and 'cheap-flight, weekend-break' tourism. These activities may not reflect the loftier aspirations of Habermas but the consumer-driven identities that have emerged are not automatically disconnected from larger values and principles. The often tawdry and over-commercialised world of sport – and especially football – provides an excellent example of a popular activity that creates a powerful sense of Europe as an everyday space of sporting contact and competition but which is also an inspirational, romantic and heroic 'theatre of dreams'.[55]

---

[52] Several recent American commentaries have warned of the dire consequences of a resurgent, united and independent Europe in rather fearful terms. See, for example, T. R. Reid, *The United States of Europe: The New Superpower and the End of American Supremacy* (New York: Penguin, 2004) and Jeremy Rifkin, *The European Dream: How Europe's Vision of the Future is Quietly Eclipsing the American Dream* (New York: Penguin, 2004).

[53] Craig Calhoun, 'Imagining solidarity: cosmopolitanism, constitutional patriotism, and the public sphere', *Public Culture* 14, 1 (2002) pp. 147-171.

[54] Tony Judt, *Postwar: A History of Europe since 1945* (London: William Heinemann, 2005) pp. 777-800. The idea of 'banal cosmopolitanism' is discussed in Ulrich Beck, 'Cosmopolitan realism: on the distinction between cosmopolitanism in philosophy and the social sciences', *Global Networks* 4, 2 (2004) pp. 131-156. It evidently owes a great deal to Michael Billig, *Banal Nationalism* (London: Sage, 1995).

[55] A recent British newspaper report in the sports pages summed this up neatly. An Italian player was recently signed by the newly-appointed Swedish coach of an English Premier League team who had apparently sealed the agreement by insisting that the team expected 'to be in Europe next year' i.e. to qualify for one of the main European competitions. The previously reluctant player

The concept of banal cosmopolitanism might also explain the rapid acceptance of a range of other European reforms and initiatives, despite the initial controversies they generate. The introduction of the exceptionally bland euro banknotes at the beginning of 2002 is a case in point.[56] This was a momentous event, of course, and was described by one leading geographer as 'arguably the most radical political-economic and cultural transformation of space in Western Europe since the French Revolution'.[57] And yet the banknotes themselves, with their strange images of non-existent bridges and buildings, were ridiculed, especially in the Eurosceptic UK press. The decision to use images of invented locations and buildings to exemplify different styles of architecture was seen as evidence that Europe simply did not exist and had no clear identity that could be expressed without offending at least some of its constituent nation-states.[58] Despite this hostile reception, by no means limited to the UK, these curiously 'placeless' banknotes seem to have acquired a quirky appeal, quite at odds with the grand and sombre ideas their artwork was originally intended to communicate. The euro banknotes may never be loved, but who would want a society in love with its own currency? Certainly, nostalgia for the 'old' national currencies, the banknotes of which generally depicted real landscapes and real historical figures, is nowhere near as widespread as many had feared. This suggests an intriguing and surprising capacity on the part of the European public to accept that Europe is, almost by definition, a curiously placeless place, indeed perhaps the first post-national space. This does not mean that the idea of Europe has no serious moral or ethical ideals; it is simply that these ideals appear to be accepted as background

---

was quoted as saying that although he understood little English (and presumably even less Swedish), he decided to sign when he heard the single word: 'Europe'.

[56] The euro began trading on the world markets electronically at the beginning of 1999, three years before banknotes and coins were introduced in the euro-zone countries.

[57] Erik Swyngedouw, 'Authoritarian governance, power, and the politics of rescaling', *Environment and Planning D: Society and Space* 18 (2000) pp. 63-76, quotation on p. 71.

[58] Popular opposition to the euro in the UK is certainly based on a desire to maintain 'traditional' coins and banknotes bearing the familiar features of the Queen even though this practice only dates back to 1960, meaning that the present monarch is the only British head of state ever to be represented on the national currency. The introduction of the euro seems to have informed, if not directly generated, a surprising volume of research on banknotes and political identity. See, for example, Emily Gilbert and Eric Helleiner (eds.) *Nation-states and Money: The Past, Present and Future of National Currencies* (London: Routledge, 1999); Virginia Hewitt and Tim Unwin, 'Banknotes and national identity in east and central Europe', *Political Geography* 20 (2001) pp. 1005-1028; Matthias Kaelberer, 'The euro and European identity: symbols, power and the politics of European monetary union', *Review of International Studies* 30 (2004) pp. 161-178; Jane S. Pollard and James D. Sidaway, 'Editorial: Euroland – economic, cultural and political geographies', *Transactions of the Institute of British Geographers* NS 27 (2002) pp. 7-10; 2002; Marcia Pointon, 'Money and nationalism', in Geoff Cubitt (ed.) *Imagining Nations* (Manchester: Manchester University Press, 1998) pp 229-254; Pauliina Raento, Anna Hämäläinen, Hanna Ikonen and Nella Mikkonen, Striking stories: a political geography of euro coinage, *Political Geography* 23, 8 (2004) pp. 929-956.

assumptions in unfussy, even self-mocking way; in the spirit exemplified over the years by Euro-kitsch events such as the annual Eurovision song contest, originally conceived as a way of promoting the grand idea of a unified Europe, but now a gloriously funny, but deeply sympathetic, parody of that same idea.[59]

The new Europe: a question of geography

I want to argue, in conclusion, that there remains a final and fundamental conceptual flaw in the writings on a new cosmopolitan Europe, one rooted in the failure to develop a geographical imagination congruent with these ambitions. A remark made in 1996 by the US-based British historian Tony Judt hints at the nature of the problem. In Judt's view, the European debate had achieved much but left much work undone: 'Europe is no longer a geographical notion' he argued, 'but it is less than an answer'.[60] This strikes me as a deeply flawed assessment, based as it is on an excessively narrow understanding of geography. I would argue instead that Europe is less than an answer *because* its complex geographies are not yet fully understood. The belief that we can ignore Europe's geographies explains why Europe has thus far failed to become an arena for progressive political change. Until we reach such an understanding, which should include an analysis of geography's role in shaping the European idea in the past, we will never be able to imagine Europe afresh.

David Harvey's criticism of cosmopolitanism, briefly introduced in the prologue to these essays, makes substantially the same point.[61] For Harvey, the theorists of a new cosmopolitanism ignore the widening geographical divisions generated by a globalising neo-liberalism.[62] From this perspective, it is impossible to theorise a progressive, cosmopolitan Europe where these 'disruptive spatialities' exist and intensify. Any theory of the latter is incomplete without an explanation for the former. One does not need to share Harvey's Marxist analysis to perceive the force of his cautionary argument, made all the more compelling when one considers that Harvey is by no means unsympathetic to the kind of utopian idealism exemplified by much of the writing on a future cosmopolitan Europe.[63]

---

[59] Paul Allatson, '"Antes cursi que sencilla": Eurovision song contests and the kitsch-drive to Euro-unity', *Culture, Theory and Critique* 48, 1 (2007) pp. 87-98.

[60] Judt, A Grand Illusion? *op. cit.*, p. 141.

[61] David Harvey, 'Cosmopolitanism and the banality of geographical evils', *Public Culture* 12, 2 (2000) pp. 529-564.

[62] See, more generally, David Harvey, *A Brief History of Neoliberalism* (Oxford: Oxford University Press, 2005); David Harvey, *Spaces of Neoliberalization: Towards a Theory of Uneven Geographical Development. Hettner Lecture 2004* (Stuttgart: Franz Steiner Verlag, 2005).

[63] David Harvey, *Spaces of Hope* (Berkeley and Los Angeles: University of California Press, 2000).

Harvey's criticism is, I think, a warning rather than a counsel of despair. It is surely possible to think and to write creatively and critically about the emerging and sometimes unexpected spaces where a new, cosmopolitan Europe is being created in a way that both describes and facilitates progressive change.[64] Some of the works referenced in this chapter by professional geographers indicate that a new European geographical imagination is emerging that both analyses and enhances positive change. This work has uncovered the existence of an emerging Europe that is not a static, bounded space but an energising and transformative political aspiration; a place always in the process of becoming that cannot therefore exist within pre-set boundaries.[65]

For Giorgio Agamben, a Europe defined in this way would actively re-configure what space means. His Europe would be founded on 'an aterritorial or extraterritorial space in which all the (citizen and non-citizen) residents... would be in a position of exodus or refuge'. The word 'European' would mean 'the being-in-exodus of the citizen'. The traditional concept of 'the people' could re-emerge in this new European space 'that would coincide neither with any of the homogenous national territories nor with their topographical sum' but would act on both in new ways. 'In this new space', he argued, 'European cities would rediscover their ancient vocation as cities of the world by entering into a relation of reciprocal extraterritoriality'.[66]

As this implies, a future Europe might resemble a democratic version of the pre-modern Europe, a cosmopolitan Europe of complex, flexible, lightly-held and overlapping allegiances.[67] A similar point has been made recently by Talad Asad with particular reference to relations between Europe and the Islamic world, including the world of Islamic immigrants in Europe itself. While scarcely optimistic about the prospects of Muslim-Christian dialogue in Europe, Talad argues that the first step to

---

[64] This includes virtual spaces that are not earth-bound at all. See Robyn Brothers, 'The computer-mediated public sphere and the cosmopolitan ideal', *Ethics and Information Technology* 2, 2 (2000) pp. 91-97.

[65] Anssi Paasi, 'Europe as a social process and discourse: considerations of place, boundaries and identity', *European Urban and Regional Studies* 8 (2001) pp. 7-28; and, more generally, the essays in Mabel Berezin and Martin Schain (eds.) *Europe Without Borders: Remapping Territory, Citizenship, and Identity in a Transnational Age* (Baltimore: Johns Hopkins University Press, 2003); and David Campbell and Michael Shapiro (eds.) *Moral Spaces: Rethinking Ethics and World Politics* (Minneapolis: University of Minnesota Press, 1999).

[66] Giorgio Agamben, *Means Without Ends* (Minneapolis: University of Minnesota Press, 2000) pp. 23-24. This is quoted more extensively in Amin, 'Multi-ethnicity and the idea of Europe' *op. cit.*, p. 15.

[67] This idea is closely related to the notion of a 'new Medievalism' advanced many years ago by Hedley Bull, *The Anarchical Society: A Study of Order in World Politics* (New York: Columbia University Press, 1977). See also Margaret Jacobs, *Strangers Nowhere in the World: The Rise of Cosmopolitanism in Early Modern Europe* (Philadelphia: University of Pennsylvania Press, 2006); and Denis Cosgrove, 'Globalism and tolerance in early modern geography', *Annals of the Association of American Geographers* 93, 4 (2003) pp. 852-870.

a fuller and more productive understanding would be the dismantling of the abstract 'Enlightenment simple space' – what I called in chapter one 'absolute space' – in favour of an updated version of 'gothic complex space'. In Asad's view '[t]he question is not simply one of devolution or of regional integration… but of how to allow for more complicated patterns of territory, authority, and time' which would ensure multiple ways of life and not merely multiple identities.[68]

If the central argument developed in these essays is correct; if the modern idea of Europe has both reflected and been sustained by a modern European geographical imagination, a way of creating, understanding and representing space, and if this has in turn provided the intellectual rationale for the modern discipline of geography, then it follows that a radically different idea of Europe will need to rest upon an entirely different geographical imagination and, in turn, a new way of writing geography.[69] If geographers have a further contribution to make to the European debate – and I believe we have – this will be best achieved by constructing new and distinctively European geographies of a new and cosmopolitan Europe.

---

[68] Talad Asad, 'Muslims and European identity: can Europe represent Islam?' In Pagden, The Idea of Europe *op. cit.*, pp. 209-227. See also Luiza Bialasiewicz and Claudio Minca, 'Old Europe, New Europe: for a geopolitics of translation', *Area* 37, 4 (2005) pp. 365-372.

[69] On this point, see John Pickles, '"New cartographies" and the decolonization of European geographies', *Area* 37, 4 (2005) pp. 355-364.

KLAUS TSCHIRA FOUNDATION

The Klaus Tschira Foundation gGmbH

Physicist Dr. h.c. Klaus Tschira established the *Klaus Tschira Foundation* in 1995 as a not-for-profit organization designed to support research in informatics, the natural sciences, and mathematics, as well as promotion of public understanding in these sciences. Klaus Tschira's commitment to this objective was honored in 1999 with the "Deutscher Stifterpreis" by the National Association of German Foundations. Klaus Tschira is a co-founder of the SAP AG in Walldorf, one of the world's leading companies in the software industry.

The Klaus Tschira Foundation (KTF) mainly provides support for research in applied informatics, the natural sciences, and mathematics, and supports educational projects for students at public and private universities and at schools. In all its activities, KTF tries to foster public understanding for the sciences, mathematics, and informatics. The resources provided are largely used to fund projects initiated by the Foundation itself. To this end, it commissions research from institutions such as the *EML Research,* founded by Klaus Tschira. The central objective of this research institute of applied informatics is to develop new information processing systems in which the technology involved does not represent an obstacle in the perception of the user. In addition, the KTF invites applications for project funding, provided that the projects in question are in line with the central concerns of the Foundation.

The home of the Foundation is the Villa Bosch in Heidelberg, the former residence of Nobel Prize laureate for chemistry Carl Bosch (1874-1940). Carl Bosch, scientist, engineer and businessman, entered BASF in 1899 as a chemist and later became its CEO in 1919. In 1925 he was additionally appointed CEO of the then newly created IG Farbenindustrie AG and in 1935 Bosch became chairman of the supervisory board of this large chemical company. In 1937 Bosch was elected president of the Kaiser Wilhelm Gesellschaft (later Max-Planck-Gesellschaft), the premier scientific society in Germany. In his works, Bosch combined chemical and technological knowledge at its best. Between 1908 and 1913, together with Paul Alwin Mittasch, he surmounted numerous problems in the industrial synthesis of ammonia, based on the process discovered earlier by Fritz Haber (Karlsruhe, Nobel Prize for Chemistry in 1918). The Haber-Bosch-Process, as it is known, quickly became and still is the most important process for the production of ammonia. Bosch's research also influenced high-pressure synthesis of other substances. He was awarded the Nobel Prize for Chemistry in 1931, together with Friedrich Bergius.

In 1922, BASF erected a spacious country mansion and ancillary buildings in Heidelberg-Schlierbach for its CEO Carl Bosch. The villa is situated in a small park on the hillside above the river Neckar and within walking distance from the famous Heidelberg Castle. As a fine example of the style and culture of the 1920s it is considered to be one of the most beautiful buildings in Heidelberg and placed under cultural heritage protection. After the end of World War II the Villa Bosch served as domicile for high ranking military staff of the United States Army. After that, a local enterprise used the villa for several years as its headquarters. In 1967 the Süddeutsche Rundfunk, a broadcasting company, established its Studio Heidelberg here. Klaus Tschira bought the Villa Bosch as a future home for his planned foundations towards the end of 1994 and started to have the villa restored, renovated and modernised. Since mid 1997 the Villa Bosch presents itself in new splendour, combining the historic ambience of the 1920s with the latest of infrastructure and technology and ready for new challenges. The former garage situated 300 m west of the villa now houses the Carl Bosch Museum Heidelberg, founded and managed by Gerda Tschira, which is dedicated to the memory of the Nobel laureate, his life and achievements.

Text: Klaus Tschira Foundation 2007

For further information contact:

Klaus Tschira Foundation gGmbH
Villa Bosch
Schloss-Wolfsbrunnenweg 33
D-69118 Heidelberg, Germany
Tel.: (49) 6221/533-101
Fax: (49) 6221/533-199
beate.spiegel@ktf.villa-bosch.de

Public relations:
Renate Ries
Tel.: (49) 6221/533-214
Fax: (49) 6221/533-198
renate.ries@ktf.villa-bosch.de

http://www.villa-bosch.de/

PHOTOGRAPHIC
REPRESENTATIONS

Photographic representations: Hettner-Lecture 2006

Plate 1 Michael Heffernan in the *Alte Aula*.

Plate 2 & 3 Peter Comba, Vice-Rector; Klaus Tschira, President KTF.

Plate 4 Reception in the *Bel Etage*.

Plate 5 Discussion in the departmental gardens.

Plate 6 Second lecture, *Geographisches Institut.*

Plate 7 Public debate with Michael Heffernan, chaired by Matthew Hannah

Plate 8 Seminar in the studio of the *Villa Bosch*.

LIST OF PARTICIPANTS

List of participants

The following graduate students and young researchers participated in one or several of the three seminars with Michael Heffernan:

BELYAEV, Demyan; Department of Geography, Heidelberg
BUTINA, Branka; Department of Geography, Heidelberg
DORBAND, Jana; Stiftung Wissenschaft und Politik, Berlin
FILEP, Bela; Department of Geography, Berne
FREIHÖFER, Jana; Department of Geography, Heidelberg
FREYTAG, Tim; Department of Geography, Heidelberg
GLASZE, Georg; Department of Geography, Mainz
GÖPFERT, Mirco; Department of Geography, Mainz
GRÄBEL, Carsten; Modern and Contemporary History, Konstanz
JÖNS, Heike; Department of Geography, Heidelberg
KLUMPNER, Paul; Institute of Geography, Innsbruck
KOSEL, Carolin; Department of Geography, Heidelberg
LOCSEI, Hajnalka; Department of Regional Geography, Eötvös Loránd University, Budapest
MAGER, Christoph; Department of Geography, Heidelberg
MARXHAUSEN, Christiane; Department of Geography, Heidelberg
MATTISSEK, Annika; Department of Geography, Heidelberg
MEYER, Aika; Department of Geography, Mainz
MOSER, Silvia; Department of Geography, Heidelberg
ROSS, Nina; Department of Geography, Heidelberg
SAMSTAG, Kathrin; Department of Geography, Mainz
STERN, Asaf; Department of Geography, Jerusalem
TAGAI, Gergely; Department of Regional Geography, Eötvös Loránd University, Budapest
WEBER, Hans-Jörg; Department of Geography, Heidelberg
WUNDER, Edgar; Department of Geography, Heidelberg

Plate 9 Some participants of the Hettner-Lecture 2006.

Cover illustration: Abraham Ortelius: *Theatrum Orbis Terrarum* (Antwerp, 1584); The inside of the European Parliament in Brussels in January 2006 (adapted) *http://commons.wikimedia.org/wiki/Image: European-parliament-brussels-inside.JPG*, permission under the terms of the GNU Free Documentation License, Version 1.2. Photograph of Michael Heffernan by Thomas Bonn
Cover design: Tim Freytag and Volker Schniepp
All photographs in 'Photographic representations' by Thomas Bonn

Every effort has been made to obtain permission to reproduce material contained in this book. The publishers apologise for any errors or omissions and would welcome these being brought to their attention.

HETTNER-LECTURES

1 *Explorations in critical human geography* DEREK GREGORY 1997
2 *Power-geometries and the politics of space-time* DOREEN MASSEY 1998
3 *Struggles over geography: violence, freedom and development at the millennium* MICHAEL WATTS 1999
4 *Reinventing geopolitics: geographies of modern statehood* JOHN A. AGNEW 2000
5 *Science, space and hermeneutics* DAVID N. LIVINGSTONE 2001
6 *Geography, gender, and the workaday world* SUSAN HANSON 2002
7 *Institutions, incentives and communication in economic geography* MICHAEL STORPER 2003
8 *Spaces of neoliberalization: towards a theory of uneven geographical development* DAVID HARVEY 2004
9 *Geographical imagination and the authority of images* DENIS COSGROVE 2005
10 *The European geographical imagination* MICHAEL HEFFERNAN 2006

Please order from: *Franz Steiner Verlag GmbH / www.steiner-verlag.de*
Distribution by Brockhaus / Commission, Kreidlerstraße 9, D-70806 Kornwestheim
E-Mail: bestell@brocom.de Tel. 0049 (0)7154 1327-0 Fax 0049 (0)7154 1327-13